SPARKY

SPARKY

Barcelona, Bayern and Back

The autobiography of Mark Hughes

Mark Hughes
with Peter Fitton

COCKEREL BOOKS LTD

First published in Great Britain in 1989 by
Cockerel Books Ltd
23–25 Maddox Street, London W1R 9LE

ISBN 1 869914 10 4

Jacket designed by Stephen Knowlden Associates
Jacket photos (front) Steve Hale (back) Bob Thomas

Photoset in North Wales by
Derek Doyle & Associates, Mold, Clwyd.
Printed in Great Britain by
Butler & Tanner Ltd, Frome and London.

To Gran, my number one
fan

FOREWORD (1)

I have to say that if I had to choose a 'Best XI' from the players I have handled as a manager then Mark Hughes would certainly be in it. Mark is as strong a centre-forward as I think I have ever seen – he's impossible to shift when the ball's played in to him, yet for all his physical strength and power he has such a delicate touch.

I've often said that if Mark started scoring 'scruffy' goals he'd have a tally as high, if not higher, than his Welsh pal, Ian Rush. But 'scruffy' goals are not his style. Every goal credited to Mark Hughes is stamped 'quality' or 'spectacular' ... the sort of goal you would expect to see used to run with the opening credits of *Match of the Day*.

Having acknowledged the lad's talents, I have to admit that, strange as it might seem in retrospect, when I first saw him play as a Manchester United junior I wasn't greatly enamoured of his abilities.

But I remember how my opinion changed almost in a single instant during a Youth Cup match against Sunderland. Mark hadn't done much in that game, but then, late on, he suddenly burst past about four defenders and set up a great chance for Norman Whiteside.

Any doubts I had about him vanished in that moment. I thought 'this kid can be a real player.' And, of course, it didn't take him long to prove it. Once I'd given him his senior debut in a Milk Cup tie against Oxford, he was on his way, his rise remarkably rapid.

I wasn't surprised by his success. Only one thing about the career of Mark Hughes has surprised me – that he wasn't a spectacular success in Spanish football. With his strength and power, plus his natural ability, I had expected him to tear the Spanish defences apart. Perhaps his failure in that instance was due to reasons outside of football – the emotional difficulties which come with living abroad, and the struggle to settle into and adjust to a new environment.

Personally, I think he went over there too soon. I couldn't blame him for being attracted by the money and the opportunity, but I felt he might have been wiser to have waited another two years. I know I wanted him to stay at Old Trafford.

However, he went and he learned, and I've no doubt he came back a wiser young man. In football, as in life, you have to do what you think is right at any given time. It's all part of the growing process, you can only learn from experience, and if you don't accept a challenge when it presents itself you can never know what you might have done.

Mark has already given a lot of people a lot of marvellous memories of some wonderful goals, and I'll wager he'll produce a few more before he's finished. The story told in this book is only the beginning, but what a fascinating beginning!

Ron Atkinson
Manager, Sheffield Wednesday FC
September 1989

FOREWORD (2)

When I signed Mark Hughes to Barcelona I saw in him a player of great potential, a spectacular goal-scorer and a young man who might well thrive in the huge Nou Camp stadium. In his very early twenties, he was undoubtedly young at the time – did that make it any more of a gamble to lift him out of the English game and put him down in the Spanish one? I don't think so.

Whatever walk of life you are in, moving to live and work abroad is a big step – you can never know until you try it just how you will react. This is the same for footballers as for anyone else, and for the team manager it is impossible to know exactly how any one player will handle the situation. Certainly, you can check out the footballing side of things to the *nth* degree, but on the personal, private side, you just have to take a bit of a leap in the dark.

Barcelona, for Mark, turned out to be a less than happy episode, as is recorded here, but neither he nor any of us involved, could have predicted that. Comparing his experience with Gary Lineker's illustrates the two sides of the coin, as far as playing abroad goes. These two very different players, with contrasting personalities, get along very well together – yet one took to the foreign environment and developed within it, while for the other the change of scene served as a negative backdrop, from which emerged his positive desire to get back home.

Once home, Mark's talent flourished and he has continually proved what a great asset he is to a team – both for Manchester United and, at national level, for Wales. He is one of the most acrobatic and exciting strikers in the game and I am positive that there is even more potential to be realised. I look forward to watching that process and wish Mark every success.

Terry Venables
Manager, Tottentham Hotspur FC
October 1989

CHAPTER ONE

'Old Lager Legs'

They plucked Sparky from the pages of a schoolboy comic and presented me with a nickname for life. It's stuck with me from my first kids' kick-about in the Welsh valleys right through a career climb involving three of the world's most famous football clubs, Manchester United, Barcelona and Bayern Munich.

But, with a little more than a chuckle of self-relief, I have to confess that in those days they might have been smarter to have called me ... Sparkout. That description would have been more appropriate and much closer to the secret nickname I had for myself in the early days at Old Trafford. 'Old Lager Legs' was the pet handle. And if that doesn't give the game away nothing will.

The truth is that when the foreigners first came chasing and fame began to beckon I was putting away pints faster than First Division opponents. No, I was never threatening the legendary performances of Jimmy Greaves in the unofficial boozers' league, and I've very definitely conquered the problem now. But at the time there could be only one description of my preparation for the world of pro football ... sheer lunacy. It just couldn't last. And, more to the point, neither could I.

I am under no illusions. Without breaking my high jinks lifestyle by moving abroad I could have been doomed. Certainly I would never have been in shape, neither physically nor mentally, to have claimed the 1988–89 players' Player of the Year award. Maybe, just maybe, I wouldn't have made a player at all. And that's the most chilling bottom line of the lot.

The lure of the local, the pull of the pint – call it what you want – might have wrecked everything. At the time I just didn't recognise the dangers, or possible damage, to my firmly held ambitions. For me it was an ice breaker. A ready-made method for dealing with the pressures of trying to make it when, in my own mind at least, I appeared more of a candidate for the scrapheap than stardom.

The boozing game started when I was just seventeen and it never even entered my head that I was at risk. It was an escape route, a run for cover. I was raw, introverted, homesick and with one objective in mind. To get back to Ruabon, my home village in Wales, and pals I had known since I first climbed out of the pram. And go back I did. Fast and often.

At first it was simply a down-the-local thrash with my mates. Brilliant at the time, too. Every weekend I would get wrecked, absolutely legless. Next stage was the big league in Manchester and tangling with a wild bunch self-acclaimed as the Dirty Dozen. I bumped into them on holiday and from the first day I strongly suspected their cash came from a brewery profit-sharing scheme! Finally, and the biggest nightmare of the lot, was the last six months at Old Trafford before reluctantly packing my bags for Barcelona. I spent virtually every night downing my sorrows. It was mad but I felt trapped: in the end I just didn't want to go.

Only one night was kept sacred – the night before a United game. Wisely I kept that pledge and never budged from it. For the rest of the time it was pints galore, attempting to blot out what was happening to me – although the bar-room high jinks had started at least four years earlier, and for very different reasons.

As soon as the whistle went on United's junior games I couldn't sling the old size nines into the corner fast enough. Grabbing a bath was little more than a walk on water. Then came the lung-burster for the nearest station and the fastest rattler back home.

Next stop: oblivion. All my buddies – the kids from round the corner and classmates from school – were used to it. They were at it most nights of the week anyway and if fate had placed me on a building site instead of in football boots it would have been fine.

And that's where I made my first mistake. I tried to keep up with them. It was suicide. One pint led to another. Six led to seven and after that you aren't capable of counting. Yet I lapped it up. After a while I was actually waiting for them to turn up to hit the booze trail. Saturday night, seven o'clock sharp, I was ready for the action. We would sink a few and then tumble round the village for a pub crawl. Next was a club or disco in Wrexham, the curry shop and, bleary-eyed, I hit the sack about three or four in the morning.

Sunday, lovely Sunday, wasn't much different either. Except that I had to make the lunchtime session as well for a few games of pool. Really, I did my brains in like the rest of the lads. Only trouble was, I earned my living playing football, they didn't.

By Monday morning and the first training workout of the week I looked like something the cat had dragged in from the cold. Innocently, because I couldn't detect the stale ale on my breath, I didn't think anyone else could. I blithely believed I was getting away with it, but they must have rumbled me. When you've been downing the pints the night before there's only one result ... I must have stunk like a brewery on the move. Perhaps they should have had a word or two sooner because it was some considerable time before I was disciplined at United for hitting the hard stuff.

Certainly it was already having a significant effect on me. For the first two days of the week I felt terrible. I just put it down to the lame excuse that I'd always been a poor trainer. When the legs felt the strain it was because I was carrying a knock, or had a bit of a cold. Not once, no never, did it even cross my mind that I might be feeling ropey because I had hit the bar too often. The stark truth of that only penetrated the grey matter years later when I was playing abroad.

It was then I realised for the first time the benefits of staying off the booze completely, even if for me it had never got beyond the beer stakes. All of a sudden I felt fit, sharp, alive. And that's why I take real care these days. But it's difficult to have that kind of perspective – common sense if you like – when you are just a kid and all your pals are turning life into a party. Particularly when the pressure is on.

· SPARKY ·

All my life it had bugged me deep down what people might think of me. I've grown out of it quite naturally by now, but in my teenage years it was a real hang-up. And it would have destroyed me if for even a split second my back-street buddies had got the wrong impression. You know the sort of thing … 'he's off to United and suddenly he's a big shot; doesn't want to know the gang any more.' Bracket me like that and I would have hated it. So I deliberately stayed close to the family roots. And that, inevitably, put me firmly on the invited list for the weekend blow-outs. Mind you I didn't exactly put in any letters of protest about it at the time.

Far more of a concern than getting plastered was my playing future at United. I felt decidedly uneasy about my position, which probably also explained why I kept my links close to home and sought refuge there. It was quite definitely an uncomfortable pressure. Deep in my heart I realised I wasn't setting the place alight at United. To be truthful I was scrambling to secure even a place in the junior ranks, the A and B teams. But with a drink inside to reinforce the self-confidence, the problem was suddenly solved. I fully realise now that that creates a trap in itself. At the time though it was a protective barrier.

The booze was an ice-breaker for me as well. For years I could never join in with social conversation – unless it was with my blood brother! Once I hit town with the wild bunch, loaded up with a few beers, it was no sweat. OK, I wasn't exactly Bernard Manning, the life and soul of the party, but I did get involved in the chat.

Inevitably, though, there had to be a price to pay. And there was. My days as a secret boozer were eventually exposed … at the club. Others might have noticed before and turned a blind eye, but Ron Atkinson copped me more than once and delivered the hard word. I was never fined but he did carpet me in his office twice and warned of serious consequences if it happened again. The first time I was shopped by an outsider calling Old Trafford. He claimed he had seen me wrecked in a town centre pub and wanted to teach me a lesson. The truth is that on that particular occasion I was totally innocent. He had fingered the wrong man. But it was hardly rough justice … I had got away with it on so many other occasions I couldn't really feel aggrieved. And it was about that time the penny dropped. For a couple of years I'd lived it up in the style of so many other teenage kids, blithely unaware of the consequences of booze. Now I was paying the price.

Nothing sinister, nothing serious, but the first signs were there for sure. Getting blitzed at weekends and stocking up with one or two more during the week had to catch up I suppose. When I was having a few back in Wales, the rest of the week I was on the wagon, so by the time Saturday kick-off came round the drink was out of the system. Once I started having a couple of pints mid-week things really started to slide. If you have a little bit of a hangover piling into training in mid-week it's bound to show. And it did.

At the time my club digs were on the training ground doorstep. At most my bedroom was 100 yards from the touchline. So after a couple of pints the night before, I wasn't exactly clambering out of bed at the crack of dawn. I would allow myself about 45 seconds flat to make the reporting deadline. Imagine how I felt: lousy. I would join the rest of the first-team squad and take up my usual position ... trying to duck the coach's scrutiny right at the back of the pack.

Admittedly, I had never been the most athletic long-distance runner in the club. I just wasn't built for it. But by this time the rest of the lads were really into taking the mickey. The fact that I liked a pint wasn't exactly a state secret and they really revved it up. Training had always been an ordeal. Now, I've got to confess, surviving a session was for me like an exercise in cleansing the conscience. I would just do enough to get through without carrying the risk of being hauled back for extra hard labour.

But when you don't put in the graft in the weekday workouts there has to be a penalty. It catches up fast and it did with me. When the big game started and I launched into my first attacking run, sometimes I discovered there was just nothing in the tank. Quietly, I would mutter to myself, this is it ... 'Old Lager Legs' is at it. The booze, without doubt, was taking it's toll. I wouldn't accept it fully until much later, but deep down I knew what was happening.

I was being naïve, stupid even, revelling in a lifestyle that was the worst possible preparation for making it to the top in soccer. But, crazy as it sounds, instead of pulling back and sobering up I did just the opposite. Increasingly I was out in the evenings – drinking. The worse I felt I was getting on at United, the more I tried to escape everything – it was a downward spiral and I didn't know how to stop it. It became particularly bad as preparations for my move to Barcelona took shape. The only excuse I can plead now is that I was tortured and tormented by the idea of quitting English football.

In the final six months at United before heading off to Spain I was living a nightmare. I hardly spent an evening without hitting a bar somewhere in town. That's when the boozing got a bit too serious and it was undoubtedly closely linked to the transfer developments and the daily speculation of a £2 million move.

Fans, the Press, even people in the corner shop, were pestering me about what was going to happen at the end of the season. All I could do was keep a straight face and bluff. I denied all knowledge of Barcelona's negotiations, although through it all I knew I was on my way out.

Then the phone calls started. Nightly, non-stop, they called me at my digs. Italian waiters from Birmingham or somewhere had got the number. They were acting as agents for Juventus, Milan or whoever, they claimed, and was I interested in moving to Italy? Naturally, in the first few weeks, I was flattered. My ego was being polished very nicely thank-you. I didn't want to scare them off so I kept them happy and talked. Later it drove me crackers and I had to get out. The perfect escape route was ... the two pubs just up the road.

You could call it a vicious circle, or maybe a merry-go-round would be better. The simple fact was that my last few months virtually turned into a one-man beer festival. I was on the town most nights of the week. Right up to Thursday it was a case of anything goes. But on the eve of the match I kept to my golden rule and stayed home. It was a self-applied law which, I'm glad to say, I never broke despite the gnawing desperation I suffered at the time.

14

During that phase of my life, when the rest of the football world was buzzing with the stories of the golden jackpot that would set me up for life, I was absolutely sick. I couldn't have felt more sorry for myself if I tried. Burning a hole in me was the fact that basically I didn't want to leave. My mind was in a turmoil. I was scoring goals, making the headlines, but Barcelona beckoned. As far as I was concerned, I was just discovering what life was all about. My eyes were being opened. My heart was in Manchester, but it seemed increasingly likely that my future would be in Barcelona.

The gloom and despondency were only added to by the hassle coming my way for United's sudden and dramatic decline on the pitch. It was as if I had been branded once it was officially announced that the transfer to Spain was rubber-stamped. Fingers were quite blatantly pointed in my direction. I was the individual clearly singled out to carry the can, whether I liked it or not. The fans on the United terraces had made me their hero when we were roaring up the First Division a few months before. I had been knocking in the goals – in the early weeks of the campaign I was rapidly sweeping towards double figures – and championship talk filled the city for the first time in two decades. The football was sweet, the opposition were being mauled and flattened.

Before we knew it Atkinson's United had a ten point lead. The rest could forget it, roared the media, the race was over. But then came the slump and I ended up as the whipping boy. Because I was on my way to Barcelona, I was the obvious target for any public flak. They muttered that I didn't care any more, I was off to make a fortune and that was all that mattered. It was like having a knife twisted in my guts. Nothing could have been further from the truth. I have never walked on to a football pitch in my life and not tried. It's just not in my nature to behave that way. And I was very definitely giving United everything I had got right to the bitter end.

The real reasons for our fade-out in pursuit of the title couldn't be placed at the feet of a single individual. It was a collective failure that stemmed from a massive injury list. Don't forget that in

15

a few short but critical weeks we lost Bryan Robson, Gordon Strachan, Norman Whiteside, Remi Moses and without them we couldn't maintain the winning tempo. We lost our rhythm and, even when the casualties came back, it never returned.

However, trying to convince angry, disillusioned fans of that fact when they see you as a deserter is not exactly easy. No question, quite a few supporters pinned the blame firmly on me. I suspect some of them still do and no amount of protesting from me is going to alter the situation. All I argue is that in those traumatic final weeks before I packed my bags and left, nothing hurt me more. I felt cornered, as if everything was unjustly being tossed in my direction. I was just a convenient scapegoat and if the Barcelona episode had never happened, it wouldn't have made one scrap of difference to the outcome of that particular championship. Once Robbo and the rest were laid up, the odds were always stacked against us.

Certainly, though, the resentment I experienced drove me back again and again to drink. In plain language, I went out to drown my sorrows. Night after night after night. I wanted to banish the whole nightmare from my brain and booze appeared the best way of doing it. I don't take any pride in making that admission. It's not a boast, just a statement of fact. For even at that stage, when I was smashing back more than I had ever done before, I never considered it was having the wrong effect on my football.

It just didn't enter my head; I always had other alibis if the goals dried up or I failed to perform to expectations. Now, looking back on those madcap days, I can only accept the real truth. The alcohol must have had a detrimental effect on my football. Only a fool would suggest it didn't. Copping out in training, maybe carrying a couple of pounds extra weight, is bound to be a handicap when you rely on physical fitness to be competent at your job. And that's what going abroad taught me.

Foreign players are more disciplined about their training, they don't try to skive. Instead they work flat out through the whole session, fully aware that they will get the benefit when the real game kicks off. I soon learned the secret from them in Spain.

Also, vitally, just moving there broke the boozing pattern for me. My old sparring partners were left behind and at Barcelona I soon met a new buddy – England striker Gary Lineker. Even from long range you can see he's not exactly a bar fly. His favourite idea of an enjoyable night out is a glass of wine over a restaurant dinner. So suddenly I was out of boozing pals and I can't say it broke my heart.

Long-term the change in life style suited me fine. But that phase of my career didn't pass without one final hiccup, if you'll pardon the expression. And that was when a mate from Wales plonked himself on my Spanish doorstep one morning. By that stage I had become such a recluse I needed the local A to Z to find the bar nearest to my apartment. Honest. But I was also bombed out of the Barcelona first team and feeling a bit depressed about the whole transfer business.

You've guessed it – we went out and sank a few San Miguels between us. Over there nothing moves until well gone midnight and it was into the early hours before we packed it in. Predictably, the following morning I never even got close to making training. I rang the club and told a white lie. I was laid up with a cold. But the Spanish Press don't miss a trick. They had the perfect headline waiting for me 24 hours later ...

MARK HUGHES MISSES TRAINING: CATCHES COLD IN DISCO.

I can chuckle about it now, but that piece of sporting type really amounts to the perfect epitaph on my life as a full-time footballer and part-time boozer. I shall remember it forever as the turning point.

These days I'm much happier at home with my wife Jill and son Alex. I don't need any club curfews to keep me out of the boozer; they do the trick better than any rule. But Jill did have a few reservations about my return to Old Trafford from Bayern Munich in the summer of 1988. She didn't breathe a word about them at the time because she didn't want to influence my decision to return home.

Later though, she did confide in me her concern about building a future in Manchester, so close to all my old boozing haunts. She worried, naturally I believe, that I might be tempted back into my old ways. The reason was obvious. Not to put too fine a point on the situation, Jill had seen me at my worst. I met her just five months before the Barcelona transfer, slap bang in the middle of my booziest exploits. No wonder she was secretly alarmed at setting up home back in the area again. But I knew there was nothing to fear. Those days are long gone. Barcelona may have taught me a lot of painful lessons, but it also presented me with the best break of my career – a break from the booze.

CHAPTER TWO

The Barcelona Experience

There is only one way to describe the Barcelona experience: for the most part it was a full-blown, X-rated horror story – but it still had a brilliant silver lining in the script for me. No secrets ... it was money. Bundles of it. And I don't mind admitting that was, in the end, the basic driving force that got me to Spain. Nothing else would have booked me on the plane.

So many British footballers, given the opportunity to play abroad, tell the world it's for all kinds of different reasons. They need a new challenge, they have built their dreams on playing in Europe, they want to develop their technique and talent with the continentals. Maybe, but they're only half-truths. The real motivation is money. And that makes them football mercenaries just like me. There is no shame or disgrace in that – it's all about securing yourself and your family, making sure the future is financially sound for the rest of your life. And if you are able to do that kicking a ball around a football field, that's perfect.

I have no illusions on that score. Football is probably the activity I'm going to be best at no matter what I attempt outside it in the years to come. So I must make it count. But from first word to last the Barcelona episode could have unbuckled me and my career ambitions. And I'm prepared to shoulder some of the responsibilities for what happened. It was all linked to a breakdown in communications between United and me.

The whole business started with an innocent mix-up. At the time I was picking up just £200 a week. Not much for a so-called 'star' lucky enough to be grabbing the headlines and glory at one of the world's most famous clubs. But I wasn't grumbling. The size of the pay packet was a legacy from my days in the reserves. It just hadn't caught up with my meteoric rise and I was clearly miles adrift of the other first team players in the earning stakes.

When the club started haggling over a new contract I was very naïve about that kind of negotiating. I figured it was best to stall and play for time. Anyway, I still had roughly 18 months remaining on my present deal. I wasn't in a rush – I just wanted the real money, the right rewards. From the way things developed, the club must have read the whole situation the wrong way. I can only assume now that they were convinced I had been strongly tapped by Barcelona, or some other foreign club.

Understandably, they wanted to protect their own interests and guard against me clearing off on the cheap. In their minds, persuaded by my stubborn refusal to agree a new deal, there could be only one conclusion: I would be off to foreign football when I was free to make a fortune. If I had disappeared under my old contract – based on the Continental system of wages and age determining the transfer price – I would have gone for buttons. They couldn't allow that to happen, but it really was a case of crossed wires. It hadn't even entered my head at that stage to get on my bike in search of suitcases of pesetas. All I wanted was to stay at United and underpin my future on a *REAL* first team contract.

Honestly, if the board or the manager, had approached me with the kind of money the other top names were collecting I would have snatched their hands off. Barcelona, or anybody else for that matter, could have taken a running jump. But the crucial breakthrough in talks never happened, largely because I kept my mouth closed. I'm not the type to go in laying down the law and making demands. Consequently the people that mattered never got the real message ... that, given a choice I would stay put at Old Trafford. The inevitable happened. I never felt I was being pushed towards the exit door against my wishes, but I was on my way to Spain before I genuinely understood what was involved – and before I had ever really said 'yes'.

20

Even in the early phase of discussions I was never completely sold on the idea. Obviously I understood right away that it would be tremendous for me financially, but I never stopped questioning whether it was such a golden opportunity in the football sense. I was completely overtaken by events and made the fatal mistake, when the move was first mentioned, of not putting my foot down and declaring: 'I'm not leaving this place until I'm good and ready.'

True enough, when the foreigners first came in, I was flattered. I loved all the drama and speculation. It was like a fairy-tale. I had barely been in the game five minutes. Virtually overnight, or so it seemed, I was top of the wanted pile at one of the biggest clubs in world football. It was like being on a rocket ride and I was the wide-eyed kid. But very quickly I was focusing on another reality and the whole dimension of what I was doing began to dawn. Within weeks of endorsing that transfer option to Barcelona in January 1986 I was getting cold feet.

At the secret signing ceremony nothing seemed real. The planned move to Spain looked years away, instead of just five months. I never thought the departure date would arrive and, anyway, I reckoned something would crop up to kill the deal stone dead. As I ticked the weeks away in a personal countdown to a future I didn't want to arrive, I became more and more depressed. Desperately I prayed that Barcelona would decide against taking up their transfer option. Every day I lived in hope. Couldn't something, somebody, anything, rescue me before it was too late? My life in Manchester was knitting together very nicely, thank you, and I was extremely reluctant to walk out on it. I would have willingly given up the promised package of a fortune to stay.

Even on the July day I packed the bags and drove to Ringway Airport with my girlfriend Jill – now my wife – and the rest of my family for the big farewell scene nothing seemed real. At that stage there was no way out, I knew that, but it was like being in a dream world.

The nightmare was just three hours away, not long after the aircraft's wheels touched down on the tarmac in Spain in fact.

Sure enough the normal club welcoming party was waiting – but what happened next didn't appear anything like normal to me. It must have been an omen. They rushed me into town through Barcelona's rat-race traffic, but my senses quickly caught up. Just as soon as they dropped me at the hotel to be exact. What a dump. It was like something out of those holiday horror stories.

You couldn't have swung a cat round in the room. The so-called 'restaurant' would have been disowned by British Rail. The normal amenities were dragged from the dark ages – and this was to be my home for the next three months. Just one thought flashed repeatedly across my mind ... what the hell am I playing at, I should be on the next plane home. But there was no escape. I had no car for a start. Over the next few weeks I coughed up roughly a grand to hire one just so I could get around and make my way to training. I'm not complaining about the cash – let's be fair, they were paying me in telephone numbers to start with – but it was one of the simple touches that Barcelona didn't understand in dealing with players. They fork out enough to finance a Third World country in constructing a team and then make you feel as though you've been forgotten, banished almost.

For a while I naturally felt lost. Because the hotel food was so lousy I would tramp the city streets every night trying to find a decent place to eat. No immediate friends, no language, it was all a bit disheartening. It was the loneliest period of my life. But that's the usual routine with the Spanish clubs, I've since discovered. Their attitude is that they have signed you on a fat contract and that is the end of their responsibility. You are treated like property. They own you lock, stock and barrel.

And don't you know it.

A few weeks after my arrival they made the big concession: I got a sponsored club car. You could have parked it in a dog kennel. It looked like a matchbox model to me, but it felt bloody marvellous. At least I could get around town and go places. Not long afterwards I escaped the hotel horrors as well. I hunted far and wide and bought my own pad. It was brilliant, high in the magnificent hills above Barcelona. A typical Spanish villa was mine at last and I figured I had really done the business.

The views were spectacular. Across the windows were those characteristic wrought-iron bars they love in that part of the world. I didn't think about it at the time, but later the irony sank in. It was to develop into something of a prison over the next few months of increasing misery. In the end I *was* just like a recluse. The other players always disappeared in different directions after training. Nobody stuck around for a chat or a bite to eat. So I piled into the car and headed back home to lock myself away until the following day.

To shut out the boredom I slept most of the time. Hour after hour. I was the original Siesta Sam. The rest of the time I developed into the best toasted sandwich chef in the northern hemisphere – I could have written a cookery book on the art. It was the only food I had for days on end. Just to put the record straight, my new playing buddy Gary Lineker and his wife Michelle tried to help me as much as possible. They invited me out to dinner or round to their house. I was always grateful but umpteen times I turned them down. It just didn't seem fair. They were a young couple, not long married. And they didn't need me hogging their spare, recreational hours all the time. I don't like sticking my nose in, even when invited, so I stayed behind locked doors and snored my life away.

People have suggested since that I was just too young to cope with the different pressures and changes brought by living abroad. The flip side of the coin is that I've sampled a vital experience abroad and still returned to rebuild my British career at 25. If I had left it later that might not have been possible.

But I accept that being alone definitely didn't help. I'm sure if I had been married, with Jill along to ease the strain, that would have been a major help when the screw began to turn. What I didn't realise at the time was that she was having an equally uncomfortable experience back in Wales – and she didn't even play the game! Because I was pulling the wrong sort of media attention she got part of the reaction at home. She had never been used to the jabbing fingers of people in the street pointing her out because she was associated with me. Rather than suffer the aggravation she stayed indoors. Crazy. Just consider – a thousand miles apart and both of us living like a couple of hermits!

It wasn't always like that. Not for the first few weeks in Barcelona at least! Initially, apart from the dodgy digs, life seemed very sweet. The training sessions went smoothly and the pre-season workout matches were a dream. I was knocking in the goals and the crowd loved it. They were crowning me as the newly arrived hero. I was never that cocky that I considered I had cracked it, but the heartache and frustration to come never entered my head. I was flying. But within a few short weeks I came crashing to earth like a downed bomber.

My mate Links had been revelling in his England form, rattling the net with a few early goals to launch Barcelona's season in spectacular fashion. Me – I was already in trouble as I struggled to match his strike rate. It was a month before I broke the League jinx – and already the whisperers were at it. Then we played Real Madrid – they are treated like aliens from another planet in Barcelona – and all hell broke loose. I couldn't believe the reaction of the media. It seemed I was the star to be sacrificed. And the season was barely six weeks old.

They attacked me, some of them quite viciously, for playing my natural aggressive game. I couldn't believe what was going on. I had chased all over the park, closed down defenders to deny them space, and sweated buckets in making tackles and winning possession. That was all wiped out, dismissed, forgotten. They weren't interested in the slightest. I hadn't scored a goal, so I had to be crucified. From that first chilling reaction to my performance I reached one conclusion – you've got problems out here, old son.

And I definitely had. Maybe, no almost certainly, I had no chance of recovery from that fateful day. If they couldn't understand what my game was all about, I hadn't a prayer of surviving. All they wanted was a poacher in the box, lurking for the half chance and ready to bury it in the net. Fine, but that's definitely not me, and it never has been. Somebody had read them the wrong script – and I had to pay the penalty.

My team-mates understood totally what it was all about, they appreciated my contribution for the sake of the side. I just couldn't get the message across to the men stirring it up – the media string-pullers who only seemed satisfied with another Spanish Inquisition. They make our own Pressmen appear like pussycats. What I didn't understand in the very early stages was that it was all about football's power game off the field. And I was merely the political football being booted from one end of the field to the other.

The real target of their venom were the millionaires who control Barcelona. All they wanted was the head of the president. If they could topple him from control they would be celebrating for a month. I happened to be the best way of getting to him simply because he had sanctioned my deal. Turn the fans against me and, in a flash, you had them hostile to the man at the top.

Fortunately for me the Spanish supporters never made me a scapegoat even when things became desperate. I had no hassle in the cafes and restaurants, only sympathy and a few words of genuine comfort.

What annoyed me more than anything about the media's heavily slanted campaign was that so much bad news was being fed back for British consumption. I didn't give a damn what was splashed across the Spanish newspapers, but when the very same exaggerations and downright lies were being peddled back home it hurt deeply. That was a knife twist in the guts and I couldn't do much about it except soldier on. I was determined I wouldn't crumble or surrender under the onslaught of bad, misguided publicity. I didn't. I knew only too well I was being branded as a foreign flop and privately I fixed it in my mind not to return home until I had wiped out that kind of insult once and for all.

I had to change countries to do it, swopping Barcelona for Germany's Bayern Munich, but I'm glad I kept that promise to myself. There's no question that when a few problems build into a landslide it can bury you for all time. In black spells all kinds of doubts undermined my self belief; whether I was good enough, whether I had ever been good enough at any time. All the time you try and shut your mind to those kind of fears. It's not easy, but they must be conquered otherwise you are doomed – a candidate for the scrap heap. Once the confidence cracks you are in really serious trouble.

25

The vital motivation that drove me on was to make certain I wasn't dismissed as a write-off ... another footballing export who wasn't capable of handling the very different pressures of playing abroad. It would have been so tempting to do a runner. Barely three or four months into my contract that thought very definitely crossed my mind. But you just can't bottle out because times are bad.

I always knew, the whole time I was in Spain, that I didn't do myself justice. No question, I could have performed a lot better than I did. But my clubmates realised the ordeal to which I was being subjected. Always, they backed me to the hilt and encouraged me to battle on. So did Terry Venables. Let's not forget his head was on the block as well. He had been convinced I was up to the job out there and, in the final analysis, I have got to accept the bottom line that I wasn't. In the circumstances he did as well for me as he possibly could. Never once did he shrink from being totally supportive and he was very much in the crossfire when personal loyalty was tested to the limit.

Not only were the Press sniping at him for the huge investment in me, there inevitably had to be pressure from above as well. But he stood by me as long as he possibly could. Anyone else would have jettisoned me a lot sooner – Terry was always ready with the comforting arm. He called me into his office, or pulled me on the training ground, on countless occasions in an attempt to protect me from what was going on. He asked me if I wanted a short break from football so I could get home to re-charge the batteries.

Once again though I let things drift. Predictably, I was prepared to suffer in silence, but I don't suppose you can change your basic character. It was my style and I had to live with it. If I could have opened my heart, I now realise it could have been of significant help. I should have knocked on Terry's door, revealed all my troubles and worries, and then emphasised: I need help. At that stage it just might have resolved the whole situation, but I never did. And so I had to endure it all for a few more months.

I made a few trips back home to get away from the aggro and it was while I was in Wales that the message was fed through to me that Alex Ferguson, who hadn't long been in charge back at United following Ron Atkinson's sacking, would take me back at the first opportunity. It was the best news I had had in ages. At least it seemed that someone wanted me! But that solution was still a long way over the horizon. We were well into March – 10 months after I had joined Barcelona – when the cavalry arrived and I was left out of the team on a permanent basis.

I knew the writing was on the wall as we approached a very important EUFA Cup tie away to Dundee United. This was the moment of truth. We had to win in Scotland or it was well known that the powder keg would explode. We lost and most of the shrapnel flew in my direction. They slaughtered me. Once again it was for my approach to the game. Because I got stuck in and tackled a few opponents, it seemed to infuriate the Spanish critics. All they wanted was the back of the net bulging, which was fair enough, but I copped the needle because they didn't give me any credit for the rest of my contribution to the side.

By this stage, too, back in the League games I was increasingly being targeted by referees. They were clamping down on me for the slightest thing. They considered I was playing it too rough but, in all honesty, I know I wasn't overstepping the mark.

The trouble was that the whole Barcelona team were being forced to pay a heavy price, too. The beady eye of officialdom was focused very firmly in my area of the field and because of this everyone was coming under scrutiny. I felt, in the best interests of everyone, it was better that I bowed out. So when the gaffer called me in after the EUFA Cup tie disaster I knew what to expect. Once again he asked how I was feeling and did I fancy a rest from the front line. I reckoned it might be as good a time as any to get out. But I genuinely believed it would be for only a couple of matches.

It was a few days before the penny dropped. They summoned Steve Archibald from the sticks to take my place alongside Gary. Next step, Barcelona cancelled my playing registration with the League and that prevented me playing in the First Division until the end of the season. Effectively it meant I was bombed out. And that very definitely bit deep and upset me. I was angry, too, but that was balanced by an overwhelming feeling of relief, so I didn't go bouncing in to make a song and dance about the whole affair.

The summer should have been the time for the healing process to get under way. But by the time the next campaign loomed there was another political storm brewing on the horizon. Berndt Schuster, the great German midfield player, had emerged from a heavyweight battle with the club and was back in favour. That development put my nose out of joint even further. I knew then it wasn't just a threat, it was the end of the road for me. And yet I had a contractual commitment to Barcelona well into the nineties. On that point, from the outset, they made it very plain they were prepared to honour their part of the deal. I could sit things out in the reserve team for the next seven years collecting the wages – and wasting away. I knew they meant it, too, after witnessing the experience of Schuster a year earlier.

They also understood, however, that there was no way I would accept those sort of conditions, no matter how much cash was on the line. Accept it and that was the end of my career. Over and done with at 23 – no way. By the time I got back to Britain I would be thirty and who would want me then? Within a short time I decided to cut my losses and escape. The first priority was to negotiate a sell-off price with Barcelona, then get down to the business of finding a club to take me while I thrashed out the financial side. Everton had made a few interested noises, so had Spurs and Glasgow Rangers, but United soon declared their hand. They wanted me back in Manchester in the November of 1987 and I was ready to jump on the first plane.

I met both the chairman, Martin Edwards, and the manager for a secret meeting. We talked long and hard with a handful of advisers on both sides. The stumbling block was obvious – the Inland Revenue. If I had returned at that stage it would have cost me tens of thousands of pounds in tax. I hadn't been abroad long enough to be exempt from the original deal agreed with Barcelona. I was freed from the nightmare – but the dream of returning to Old Trafford was committed to cold storage.

CHAPTER THREE
Bayern Munich

The German jokers of Bayern Munich robbed me of money in training, took the mickey out of me unmercifully, and also put a smile back on the face that had worn a frown for a year. They did all of that and much more. In fact, they were largely responsible, in a football sense, for literally saving my life. Without their help at the right time there might never have been a career revival.

I had been in the Bavarian capital only a matter of days when the mickey-taking started and the money began disappearing fast into the pockets of my new team-mates. But it didn't bother me all that much – I was ready for a laugh after all the heartache.

They set me up as the fall-guy in the first few training sessions. By now you've probably got the idea of my favourite workout. Maybe a 20-yard jog and then grab a ball for a few blasts at the nearest keeper. But after seeing me blazing a few over the bar they roped me in to their routines. Their favourite was a keep-ball exercise in which you had to make sure you kept the ball off the deck in little passing moves. Rapidly, they sussed out it was not my greatest strength. To put it mildly, the whole thing drove me barmy. And it cost me plenty, too. The rest were red hot but I always got the awkward ball – deliberately. Once I let it drop there was a fine to pay of around ten deutschmarks. By the time the day of reckoning arrived I was handing over roughly £120. Charming. The rest of them chipped in something like a fiver a piece. And it was all put in the kitty to fund a party. I didn't mind – that was exactly what I needed. The hermit was back in business.

Originally, though, I had been a little reluctant to join Bayern.
Once I decided to move from Barcelona on loan I realised I was
burning my boats in Spain – there was no way I would play for
them again – so everything had to be exactly right. The
temptation was United, naturally. But, as I've said, crippling
penalties on tax meant that plan had to be shelved for a few more
months. Yet I needed a secure, sensible club to rebuild a career
that might end up in ruins unless I got everything right this time.

I was torn. Just a few days before officially joining Bayern I flew
back to England in a last desperate attempt to uncover a loophole
that just might allow me to return to Old Trafford. I had talks with
both the manager and chairman and they pressed me to sign. It
was tempting. They were so persuasive in mapping out a loan
transfer drafted to make sure I had no long-term worries. In
effect, it would have meant I was back where I belonged for
good. But it would have been suicidal in its financial impact. The
personal loss would have been colossal. Tens of thousands of
pounds would literally have disappeared overnight. It was
impossible. On to Germany it had to be, full of reluctance and
fears.

Privately, at that moment, I regarded the move to Bayern as
purely killing time. Simply a way of surviving the April deadline
when the tax penalties would be gone for good. But within days it
wasn't just a money saver ... it was a lifesaver as well. I knew
immediately that German football was made for me. Tough,
competitive and the kind of playground I could make my own. It
wasn't simply a case of spectacular scrapbook goals winning you
glory. They accepted that I had other qualities to offer their game.
And just as an incidental bonus, I was back playing in the
European Cup. Suddenly, I felt like the guy on death row winning
an eleventh hour reprieve.

My debut was a doddle. There was a hard, combative edge but
I was able to pull off defenders and find space. Now this is what
Continental football is all about, I reckoned. It was a dream. One
chance came my way, I put it in the back of the net, and that was
the end of Bayer Urdingen and my baptism in the Bundesliga.
Great, I was ready for a car dash to the plane and the race back to

see Jill, who was expecting more than me: our first son Alex was on the way. However, the airport was fog-bound and I was left stranded. Uli Hoeness, the former German World Cup player and the big noise at Bayern, came to the rescue and whisked me back to his house for football tittle tattle long into the night. Before long he was calling my performance world class.

Hang on, that's a bit strong, was my immediate reaction. But at least it was a positive opinion instead of all the knocking, nightmare, negative thinking that had surrounded me at Barcelona.

In Spain I had waited four or five months to get a car. At Bayern I arrived on the Wednesday and by Friday afternoon there was a brand-new BMW snugly parked in the garage. I hadn't even kicked a ball for them at that stage. Now that's style, the simple touch that makes you feel welcome. The hotel was perfect. So was the rest of the first-class treatment. Jill flew in and joining me on the tarmac to greet her, was the boss with a bouquet of flowers for her. Nice touch again, and it counts for everything. But nothing like the staggering exercise laid on to get me in the Bayern side five days after I made my debut. Uli declared I just had to be out there on the park. Trouble was I already had a firm booking – with Wales in a vital European championship qualifier. And that, believe it or not, was in Czechoslovakia.

But Uli was adamant. He believed I had captured the imagination of the Bayern fans with that first match performance and their interest couldn't be allowed to die. Soon, he was off making dozens of phone calls. Private jets, standby cars, minute-by-minute schedules. I couldn't believe what was happening.

By Wednesday everything had been laid on. I was in Prague with the rest of the Welsh boys. We needed to win to make the finals. Sadly, it ended up another tragedy and we lost 2-0. But I wasn't in that depressed, despairing, dressing room for too long – like 30 seconds to be exact. Hustler Hoeness made sure of that. Outside engine revving, waiting to hurtle us to the airport, was ... a Lada. I'm not kidding. Through the Czech countryside we zoomed at all of 30mph, but in that heap it felt as if we were breaking the land-speed record. With loose bolts flying, and exhaust just holding on, we arrived on the runway. There, a gleaming, high roller's private jet. Bundled inside, we were airborne and heading for the German border before you could blink. But Uli still hadn't finished with the big build-up.

Over Munich the plane banked, and slid under the cloud layer. Down below us was the Bayern stadium with the match against Borussia Moenchengladbach in full swing. The pilot knew the drill ... down we went for a dramatic fly past before picking up the flight path for the airport.

We crammed into Uli's car – no not another Lada. This time we had the business, a full-blown turbo Porsche. When the gaffer put the boot down along the autobahn it was as if we hadn't stopped flying. The ground was reached before we could change underclothes twice!

Hoeness had deliberately not told any of the players, officials or the public of his secret scheme. So I was smuggled into the stadium and kept in hiding upstairs until the team had gone out for the second half. He wanted the maximum psychological impact – and he got it.

Just as I was getting changed, Borussia nicked a goal. We were behind. They rushed to get me to the touchline for the warm-up. Even then the penny hadn't dropped with the crowd. They were fooled because one of our reserve-team players was virtually a carbon copy of me. They figured it must be him. Then, up on the flashing video screen, they announced a substitution and put my name in. Nobody could believe it. I was supposed to be hundreds of miles away in Prague. It wasn't possible. And nobody was more stunned than the Borussia players.

Within five minutes we had equalised. It was a sudden-death Cup game and we were committed to extra time. Everything was wrapped up by our late winner and the place went wild. The team had pulled off a sensational victory, but the real triumph was for Herr Hoeness. Not just with the fans – but definitely with me. It's good to have the ego polished occasionally – particularly after my recent experiences – that little exercise certainly did my heart good. To consider that any club would go to such lengths for a

Aged 15 with my first Welsh Schoolboys cap

Welsh Schoolboys – featuring myself (back row 2nd right), and also Clayton Blackmore (back row far left)

In action for United, 1985

Photo: Steve Hale

Photo: Daily Mirror

Against Oxford United, September 1985   *Photo: Daily Mirror*

Ecstatic after scoring for Wales against Spain in a World Cup
qualifying match, 1985   *Photo: Steve Hale*

Photo: Daily Mirror

Signing autographs at United's training ground

In action for United against local rivals, Manchester City, in
the season before moving abroad   *Photo: Steve Hale*

Ready to go in the colours of my new club – Barcelona   *Photo: Bob Thomas*

The British connection – with Gary Lineker and Terry Venables in the Spanish sunshine

Photo: Bob Thomas

Signing autographs through the gates of Barcelona's Andorra training camp

Photo: Bob Thomas

Looking out from behind another set of gates – this time to my home

Inside – the sitting room

Photo: Bob Thomas

Domestic scenes – on the balcony and in the kitchen!

Heading for goal against FC Porto in the Gamper Tournament, August 1987

Photo: Bob Thomas

single individual player was quite staggering. It didn't just make my day, it made my season ... And almost convinced me to stay for another couple of years.

In the final months of that season a few clubs were gathering, I'm glad to say, to examine whether I could have a future with them. Most were in Britain, Rangers and Spurs were mentioned strongly but nothing really happened in negotiations. Everton's Colin Harvey, though, did declare his hand very early. He had revealed he was interested in talking over a move to Goodison Park while I was still in Spain. The stakes increased months later.

I played for Bayern against Everton as part of the League's Centenary celebrations. I did reasonably well, scoring a goal and having another disallowed. Everton must have been impressed because they got Kevin Ratcliffe, my Welsh captain, to give me a buzz. Rats jokingly said he didn't know what his club were playing at going in for me, but he had a message from the boss. At least I hope he was joking. The word, anyway, was: would I be prepared to consider further a transfer to Everton in the summer? I had options, and was always willing to consider most of them, but if I was going back home there was only one place – United. Even when I left Old Trafford, almost two years earlier, I had always fixed the fairy-tale ending in my mind: I planned to finish my career where it had all started.

The choice for me was dramatically simple. Bayern or United. Nobody else really counted if I was being absolutely honest. And the Germans were certainly tugging at the heart strings. They had rescued me, put new fight back in my football, demonstrated the value of hard, demanding physical effort on the training field. Turned my whole career round in fact. They had provided the platform to prove to a doubting world I could be a success at the very top of the profession. That was crucial. In Spain I had got so tense, burdened by worry and self-doubt, that I was looking a dummy. I couldn't even control a simple pass. It was downright embarrassing. Talk about not being able to trap a bag of cement, it was just a joke.

So naturally I felt a debt to the Germans. I also loved the lifestyle and so did my wife. We were settled, contented.

Flattered too, because even though they look after stars very well financially, they don't hit the big-money transfer trail very often. For the first time they were ready to break with tradition and pay Barcelona over a million. I was stunned. They pulled out all the stops to keep me. And I was very close to accepting the invitation. It made sense financially. In football terms there was a strong motivation too. So many people had stuck the knife in me earlier, labelling me a flop and now Bayern were handing me the opportunity to make all the critics choke on their words. In their game I knew I could be a big success.

Jill also fancied a couple of more years on the Continent. Both of us realised that returning to England at that stage meant we were going home for good. There would probably never be another chance abroad and it was very tempting to stay. Bayern's management were also sticking their necks out in their willingness to invest so much cash in my future. After all, they hadn't won anything with me in the team.

In the end, though, the rest of the cash just didn't tie in. I'm sure they were very disappointed when I gave them my decision to return to United. But there was one final, gnawing doubt that convinced me to leave. If I rejected United at this stage I might never get the chance again. For all I knew they might go out and invest in another young striker to go with Brian McClair and I couldn't take the gamble. The other important factor was Alex Ferguson himself. He seemed to me the right manager to bring success and the championship to Old Trafford. Non-stop he had kept up his commitment to sign me.

Even when I was first suffering the traumas in Spain he quietly flew out and offered some comforting words. Then in Germany he and Archie Knox, the first team coach at United, put their cards on the table and were very persuasive. The boss really impressed me with his fanaticism for football and his desire to win the pots for United. I owed it to him to give myself another crack at the glory game within a club that I believe is created for greatness in the world game. The rest is definitely up to me.

But my commitment is written on a piece of paper tucked somewhere in the club's confidential files. It's a five year contract that binds me to United until I'm 29. As far as I'm concerned it might as well be a deal for life. I've done my travelling. If the decision is left to me I'll be sticking around until I can't do the business any more – gunning for the silverware and the biggest prizes in the game.

CHAPTER FOUR

Rush, Lineker et al – partners in attack

England, Spain, Germany. They were three whistle-stop destinations in two unbelievable years that turned my whole life upside down. And there might even have been one more soccer stopover thrown in. The chance, slim though it proved, was to tackle the toughest foreign battlefield of the lot, Italy. Right in the front line, too, with Ian Rush, my international team-mate and a long-time pal off the field.

Juventus wanted to put us in the same strike force at the end of Rushy's first season out in Turin. Apparently, they believed an all Anglo combination was the answer to both our problems – and they could well have been right. There had been a few whispers, I've got to admit, when I was still at Barcelona. The word was out that mighty Juve were keen on doing a deal, but I dismissed it as just the usual newspaper banter and speculation. True enough they had a few high-powered contingents watching me when I was playing for Wales. Nothing happened officially. I suspected they were just checking me out, seeing how I operated in the same forward line as Rushy. They must have seen something they liked because they got down to the wheeler dealing in the summer of 1988.

The trouble was that by then I had already signed for United. Juventus came in just too late, only a few days after I had completed all the formalities at Old Trafford. Later I discovered that the men who usually don't take no for an answer offered United a considerable profit on what *they* had just forked out to Barcelona. I don't know what the figure was, I don't even care. But the reply was short and sweet from our boardroom – forget it. The desperately late move by Juventus was, apparently, prompted by our performance together in a so-called international friendly for Wales against Italy. We won by the solitary goal – but what a price we both had to pay.

It was brutal, a real bloodbath. I reckon the whole Italian team had heard the rumours that I was destined to play with Rushy in their League the following season. They clearly intended to kill the idea stone dead and, let me say, the Mafia couldn't have done the job better. I've never been whacked so hard in my life. High, lethal boots, flying elbows, gouging, tripping, shirt-tugging – we got their whole repertoire. It made the Spaniards appear like the local welfare services.

That said, it was not this on-field aggression which stopped me hankering after a move to join Rushy. Once United banished the idea of another deal, I was absolutely delighted. Going to Juventus would have been too much like leaping from the frying pan into the fire. The only obvious appeal would have been playing shoulder-to-shoulder with Ian in top club football. And on two other occasions that was on the drawing board – yet never happened.

Originally, Terry Venables' blueprint at Barcelona had been shaped around the two of us up front together. Apparently he wanted Rushy before chasing down that other great poacher, England's Gary Lineker. But at that stage Ian was involved in agreeing an option with Juventus. Even Barcelona, with all their fabulous wealth, couldn't compete so the double deal was doomed. Naturally Rush and myself had discussed it and both of us fancied the possibilities. But in the end, as always, money talks. Subsequently, a lot of friends and outsiders, have suggested it might have saved the pair of us from so much heartache. The benefits of playing together abroad are obvious; we could have cushioned one another against the pressure and we understand each other's game almost instinctively. Still, it's no point crying over the promised land. It didn't happen so the whole question is not worth bothering about.

During my last few weeks with Bayern the question cropped up again and this time it was Uli Hoeness picking my brains. The grapevine was full of speculation about Rushy because he had been given such a hard time in Italy. Uli believed, like Juventus, that teaming us up together might be the perfect solution. Once again the stumbling block was money. They had the scope to satisfy the player but nowhere near enough to foot the actual transfer bill. Still it was a nice idea to dream about – for me particularly. I would love to have a few years in tandem with Rushy.

He is the king of modern-day strikers, a footballer who has underlined his world-class ability at the highest level. Over here the buzz names are Maradona, Cruyff, Pele, Van Basten and the like. I can understand the way the public become transfixed by such reputations. But we must never forget that we are not able to scrutinise such giants, week in and week, out to see if they really justify our fantasies. Yet abroad, among players and fans alike, Rushy's goalscoring feats earn him the same kind of adulation. And rightly so.

Without question he is a footballer of outstanding class. Long before I hit the First Division scene Ian had been piling in goals for Liverpool at a rate of more than thirty a season. To do that on a regular basis you have to be extraordinary. In the British game he stands alone. I don't like making public judgements about personal friends but, yes, I think he is marginally better than another great footballing pal, Gary Lineker. More about that later, because first I intend to concentrate on a breakdown of Rush.

When he returned from Italy to be the spearhead of Kenny Dalglish's at Anfield, he was very unlucky. Apart from injury, he was cursed with a debilitating illness. And with the kind of game on which he bases his success that was always a very big handicap. People tend to think only of the goals he scores. They ignore his other massive contribution to any team he leads from the front. But having been alongside him dozens of times, I recognise one major quality ... his capacity to be the grafter of the side.

39

He closes down defenders as though somebody had laid a whip across his back. He never allows any rival a split-second of peace. That's how he claims so many of his strikes, straight from the blur of panic that he has created. But doing it Rushy's way demands strength and stamina. He might not have recognised how much the illness had robbed him of this great asset. If you haven't got the strength you just can't do it. Rushy never talked about his comeback problems, it's not his style. He's no bigshot, for all the fame and money, and he wants to be treated like the rest. So you never heard a moan from his direction. He just buckled down to the job and I'm convinced he will be there to terrorise the top teams in this country for another five or six years.

Knowing him, he will have his own answers to the snipers who have tried, during the last few months, to shoot him down. I recall Jimmy Greaves, who had his own troubles with hepatitis, suggesting that it badly affected his own career and that Rush and Lineker would never be the same again. Greavsie reckoned it would cost them that vital yard of pace where top hitmen do the real damage. I doubt that myself, but with the blinding acceleration that both Rushy and Links are blessed with I don't think it matters anyway. The pair of them are turbo-charged.

Just cast your mind back to Rushy in the FA Cup Final when he won it for Liverpool with two goals of the highest pedigree. OK, the marking wasn't all that hot but he produced what he does best – lurking on the shoulder of a defender before launching himself for the kill. They were the two incidents that told me we have nothing to worry about over his future. He hasn't lost the knack. In recent years many people have questioned me about why he is so lethal. I believe it's a simple trick. Most forwards like to trap and control the ball before they attempt to burgle a defence. Not Rushy. He accepts the ball in one movement. There's no delay, not even the blink of eye, and though it doesn't always look pretty, he's away before markers realise it. With his running power they never get back to him.

His other asset is his physical approach to football. I don't mean that he is a bruiser, but he makes defenders aware of his presence. For them he's Public Enemy No 1. For me this is the factor that gives him the advantage over Links, another fabulous finisher, and establishes him as the top man at his particular trade. But it is a very close run contest.

Gary's reaction to intimidation is remarkable. I have seen him take some terrible punishment without flinching or flaring up in retaliation. It says a lot about his whole laid-back approach to life. I'm just not built that way! If a hardcase defender takes more than one deliberate poke at me, I can't lie down; I have to take action. Reprisals are necessary to stop them overstepping the mark. I give Gary some verbal stick about never having been booked in the whole of his top-level career. When you remember the amount of fierce, often cynical, treatment he gets it's an amazing statistic. But he accepts that kind of thuggery on the field as a compliment. He feels if they want to stop him that badly then he must be good. And he is.

His pace is electric. I'm not exactly slow, but he can leave me for dead. Despite what's been said – a lot of it with his own encouragement – he's no slouch in the air. But Gary has one strength that is not often noticed – he tends to unbuckle the best teams in the world with his running off the ball. I don't think there is any striker on earth better at it: he's a master. Midfield creators are forced to pass to him because he knows where to be at the right time. A truly dangerous operator.

When I was at Barcelona and under the cosh Gary and his wife, Michelle, were a tremendous help. He had, naturally, to take care of himself on the field without bothering about me absolutely every second of the match because he was under pressure as well. But he sorted out the media – and the whole Spanish nation if you like – with the demolition job he did on Spain in that international in the mid-eighties. Four goals from him answered every snide question they wanted to toss in his direction. In one match he was bomb proof.

I was slightly surprised that he returned to England in the summer of 1989. He relished the approach to life on the Continent and I figured he might move on from Barcelona to France, or even Italy. To get him to Spurs Terry Venables has pulled off a shrewd piece of negotiating. With him around, banging in the goals at the rate of at least twenty a season, Tottenham must surely be on their way back after two seasons of re-grouping. Even at around one million pounds he has got to be a bargain.

On that scale, too, my United team-mate Brian McClair has got to be the steal of the decade at £850,000 in the modern, over-priced and crazy market. In my opinion he's one of the best footballers to come out of Scotland in years. The only thing he's short of is nationwide recognition. Ask any defender he has faced in the last couple of years and you will get the truth: they rate him as one of the most menacing opponents in the land. It's just the fans who don't appear to realise just how good he is. In my book Brian's exceptional.

Articulate, intelligent and very much his own man off the park, he gives the team everything he has got on it. You don't score 30-plus goals in your first season in English soccer without being loaded with all the gifts. One such gift that can be in pretty short supply, even in the pro ranks, is self-belief. Not with Brian. He can miss two, three, or four chances but he will still be showing for the fifth. And that will end up in the net. He never searches out a hiding place when things go wrong. In our first season together I accept that in some quarters eyebrows have been raised about whether it's the perfect partnership. I have no doubts. We are different types of players and that's why I'm convinced we have got what it takes.

Brian loves to roam the park. He drops deep waiting for the long, loping run to do the damage. It leaves me up front, often alone, but I don't mind that in the slightest. Physically it can be a bit tough, but I love that kind of challenge. It also places rivals in two minds, because they know I can do that side of the business as well, dropping off the cover and losing markers by drifting into midfield. Brian is naturally blessed for the job – watch him closely and you won't find anyone who can move quicker with the ball at his feet. Straight sprinters might beat him – but ask them to keep possession as well, instead of laying off a pass, and they won't be at the races.

Questions were asked about us last season (1988–89), but whenever we were allowed a consistent run together the potential was obvious. Most of the trouble came because too often Brian had to fill in the midfield positions to cover for injuries. It inevitably affected his confidence. But United have an investment in the pair of us. We are both comparatively young, with five-year contracts binding us to the club. I'm praying we stick together to frighten the life out of the rest of them in the years ahead.

In the past I've had quite a few different front-running partners at United. It can be a graveyard for strikers – but I've been lucky. The best have been on my side. In the early days it was Frank Stapleton and, I've got to confess, we didn't always see eye to eye. Let's say it was a love-hate relationship that kept us sparking on and off the field. My complaint was that Frank was a bit of a moaner. It was as if he couldn't help it. Grousing and grumbling seemed the daily recipe of his life, but it didn't go down too well with me at all, particularly when we had to play up front together.

As a reasonably young footballer, I thought all the carping was aimed in my direction and I objected to it. When you are having a bit of a rough time on the pitch the last thing you need is one of the top-liners bellyaching about it. I didn't appreciate it one little bit and, on and off the park, I let Frank know, sometimes with both barrels. I believe he should have been more supportive as I was the junior partner, and that's why we clashed a few times. Now, more mature and looking back, I realise it was Frank's own method for knocking me into shape. He was trying to help me survive by jumping on my toes now and again. I believed it was destructive then – now I realise it was constructive and done for my benefit. It was my learning process. And from Frank there were the early guidelines of always piling in the effort in training and giving a certain level of performance in matches. In the first couple of seasons at United the boss, Ron Atkinson, considered him the best striker in Europe. I wouldn't argue.

Alan Brazil, another partner of mine, never had a chance of winning that kind of accolade at United. In fact he never had a chance of achieving anything at all. The odds were impossibly stacked against him from the start. I remember playing with him in the first game of the season against Watford after his summer arrival. The crowd started giving him stick virtually from the first kick and it was very obvious, even in his very first 90 minutes for United, that he would have trouble surviving. They looked on him as a forward who had flopped at Spurs and yet had still cost us a fair amount of money. More to the point, he was keeping Norman Whiteside – a kid who had climbed through the United ranks and a hero of the terraces – out of the first team. They didn't like it one bit and immediately showed their contempt for the situation. Inside the dressing room everybody felt sorry for Alan, but I can't deny I was probably less sympathetic than the rest.

The reason was deadly simple. For him the situation was desperate but with the spotlight on poor old Brazil I was able to escape all the pressure and attention which is focused on the newcomer trying to earn a place. I was totally protected and had an easy ride in those vital early days, whereas he needed something dramatic, even sensational, to save him almost from day one. Once the goals failed to flow as well, that was his death warrant. It was tragic. He was a good player and a smashing bloke.

Alan, in his misery and despair, probably had as much impact on my career as anybody I've ever played alongside. Before he arrived I was third in line behind Frank and Norman Whiteside. With Brazil in the pack I was relegated to fourth place. But Frank was heading for hospital with a serious injury and I nicked a few more pre-season goals than the rest to force the issue ahead of big Norman. It was a rare break because he had always been at least two years ahead of me in development. Even when we played against him for the Welsh schoolboy team against Northern Ireland he was a figure of terror. Most of us were around 13 – I think he was even younger at 12 – but it was like dragging a full-grown bloke out of the nearest factory to take us on.

Even at that age being knocked around by Norman was a frightening experience. But for all his aggression and power, the big feller's got a lot more to offer. His in-built skill can be just as threatening as his physique. Already he has established himself as one of the best players around, but if he had pace as well I believe he would by now be the best midfield player in the country. It was that lack of acceleration that made certain he would have to drop back from the front line.

CHAPTER FIVE

Managers

I've collected my wages – and a few accolades as well – under some of the biggest, most dynamic men in the football business. And I've got the scars to prove it.

The men I've called 'boss' down the years have kicked me, knocked me into shape, cajoled and comforted me in their different ways of running the show. They have all had one quality in common – a motivating influence that made certain this particular rookie, nagged by serious worries that I might not make it at all, is now earning a living at the peak of the game.

Even Ron Atkinson, my manager at Manchester United, and the guvnor I always suspected never really rated me, played a huge part in my success. Then there was Terry Venables, very much his own man, who was able to shield me to a great degree during the ordeal at Barcelona and was generous enough to buy me dinner a few times along the way. Next came Alex Ferguson, a flame-thrower of a boss whose competitive personality, spirit and incredible will to win persuaded me that I must return to Old Trafford as fast as possible. And as a consistent link right through the development of my senior career there has been Mike England, the big chief at Ragbag Rovers, otherwise recognised in the international sporting arena as the Welsh national football team. More of that later.

First on the scene in my emerging years appeared Big Ron. Flamboyant, larger-than-life, and a character who probably hogged more headlines in his time at United than any of his famous players. I was never a part of his inner circle – just too young for that, I suppose – but the older players who shared a laugh and a joke with him were all very much on his side when he got the sack. They liked his football, loved his style, and they definitely didn't want to see him out of the door. In fact, the majority of the senior first team squad were very upset and angry at his dismissal. They were still convinced he could take them places.

I just didn't know him well enough, closely enough, to make that kind of judgement. But I am certain of one fact: all the image-builders were way off beam in giving the impression of a party-going, champagne-swigging, high-roller of the game. To be absolutely honest, I don't believe I ever saw him with a glass of champers except when we won a Cup Final. And then it was only for show and to be sociable. The rest of the time he was far more at home with – a pot of tea. In the end, though, I suspect that the media-created image went against him and contributed to his downfall at United. The myth put him in the dole queue for a few months.

It was okay, nobody batted an eyelid, when we were winning. But when the results started falling away the fact that he was a very up-front, outgoing personality went against him. I suppose when he first arrived at Old Trafford, back in 1981 when I was still in the kids' team, he appeared a bit flash. Maybe he felt he needed to make a big personal impact on a world-famous institution – only he would know the truth of that. But when the big man finally bit the dust, just a few months after our nightmare championship collapse, he had toned down that side of his very public personality. Talk about the track-suit boss – he lived his life in that sort of gear.

Privately, my recollection is that his favourite pastime – outside of a pot of rosie, as he called it – was taking the mickey out of the likes of me. Naturally, it didn't go down a bundle with the victim, but the other players lapped it up. What worried me most was that I was never quite certain in my own mind whether Ron was being serious, or just having a laugh. Certainly, at that stage of my career, I believed he considered me a bit of a joke as far as the first team went.

In the background I know other members of the staff were

pushing me for contention. The reserve team coach Brian Whitehouse never stopped plugging me, but Ron just didn't want to know. He didn't rate me as someone who could compete for United at the very highest level. Fair enough, he was entitled to his opinion, after all he was the gaffer. All the time he questioned my attitude and application in training. And he didn't hide the fact, either. More than once he had me in the office to lay it on the line that unless I pushed myself more I was going nowhere.

Eventually, though, he had no choice. An injury crisis forced him to call me up for a very important game. But there was still a very hard route planned before I had cracked it. At first I only got as far as the substitute's shirt. Most matches Ron would sling me on with five or ten minutes to go. It was murder. You felt more whacked with all the tension of waiting than if you had played three Wembleys on the trot.

Then came my first full-game debut. Most people remember it – Oxford in the League Cup – and I certainly won't forget it in a lifetime. Simply because I scored my first senior goal. But I'm pretty certain most folk wouldn't have a clue where I played. I was in the front line alright – as a left-winger. It's hard to imagine. Me, the wizard on the wing. Behave yourself. But at least I know if the goals dry up I can always volunteer for another job to keep my place! Oxford, I'm glad to say, was just the launching pad. I got a few more goals and then Ron had no option but to keep me in. Even if he still didn't stop taking the mickey, with me believing I was public enemy No 1.

Ron knew his football, too. He was very good at getting the message across to the troops. Not much time was spent on the opposition, but he was very straightforward and articulate about what he expected from his own men. He always counted his own strengths before he considered any rival and, in my book, that is not a bad formula for success. It was good enough for United to win two FA Cup Finals, lose in the Milk Cup to Liverpool, and launch us towards a few charges at the long-cherished championship.

The other plus factor in his management was his commitment to class operators – the footballers with a born instinct for playing the game. He didn't go in for the hammer throwers. His teams were full of entertainers – a pleasure to play in most of the time and a joy to watch. I was well established in his plans, banging in a few goals to help the cause, when United got off to the flying start that had the nation backing us for the title before Christmas. Ten straight wins – and people were falling over themselves to give us the great prize. There was only one problem. Nobody at Old Trafford, Ron and the players included, ever believed it would be that easy. And to suggest later that the manager blew it is an insult.

I can't think of one decision he made that counted to our ultimate downfall. We hit an injury pile-up, lost our way and never regained the team's initial rhythm. Plus, there was that little consideration known as Liverpool. They wound up the season with an even better run than we had started it with. So that was that. And it amounted to the first rumble in Ron's reign at United. My own situation at Barcelona had certainly complicated his long-term planning – after all I signed the option with the Spaniards in the January, mid-way through that critical season.

From that decision, the manager clearly had to look into the future knowing I would be through the door and out of the country. So he went out and bought more strikers. In came Peter Davenport and Terry Gibson. From that moment the outside world put two and two together, adding up that I was on my way. I've got to admit it, that kind of team development didn't help my own position. But you couldn't blame Ron for taking care of United's priorities and drawing up ideas for the following season.

Maybe that's why, in the closing months of that phase, I had more clashes with him than at any other time. When he started laying down the law in the dressing room over our performances I would chip in, I just wanted to say my piece. Maybe I was down in the dumps and feeling a little bit sorry for myself at the time. Naturally, my opinion wasn't always welcome, and I would get shouted down. Put simply, I tended to get my head bitten off! But on reflection I've got to say that Ron Atkinson was pretty fair, and a fair old operator in his field.

The other manager who did more than most to try and save my

neck was Terry Venables at Barcelona. You all know that was a bit of a horror story for me, but without Venners' protection it could have been a hell of a lot worse. He was always very supportive even though he was subjected to tremendous personal pressure himself. The critics were just waiting in ambush to exploit the heavy football politics at Barcelona. Their target was always the president of the club … and they knew the best way to get at him was through the team. It was the Domino Syndrome. Attack me as the foreign import to have a go at Venners and, indirectly, the man at the top of the pile who had sanctioned the whole business in the first place.

Even with that kind of burden Terry never flinched. He resisted them all and stood firm, allowing me as long as I wanted to make a go of it in the Spanish team. Only when I said I had had enough did he pull me out of the crossfire. No manager, for sure, could have given me more protection in the circumstances out there. He also tried to develop my game and mould it to the Continental style of play, but Terry really didn't have the ideal stage at Barcelona to underline his reputation as one of Britain's top coaches.

I mean, the training facilities are an absolute joke for a club of such massive status. They are squashed in under the shadow of the famous Nou Camp Stadium – a cramped, oddly-shaped piece of grass that isn't even the size of a full-size pitch. On that Terry was supposed to prepare one of the world's great teams. Madness. He had 30 top pros who all demanded a part of the action, otherwise there was war. It was more like Piccadilly Circus out on the field, absolute chaos. So he hardly had the facilities to demonstrate his technique. He undoubtedly has a vast amount of knowledge about the game. And the reputation he has for being just a Cockney Jack the Lad is way off the mark. Okay, Terry loved a laugh and a joke, but he could be deadly serious about his life and his very personal ambitions. Nobody entered his sphere of operations until he had sussed them out. He was a right old shrewdie. I'm sure he checked me out before he gave his blessing to my signing. Outside football, in his business transactions, he also always seemed to be one step ahead of the pack.

He was a bit different in his handling of players off the park as well. I've had a few right good nights out with him in Spain, even when the screw was being turned its tightest at Barcelona, and I don't reckon too may footballers have had that experience in their lives. For Terry, though, it was just normal. He would take Gary Lineker and myself out on the town. Quite a few times we went off to dinner with him at some of the smartest restaurants in Barcelona and he introduced us to the contacts and friends who could help us out there. It was his method to treat footballers as reasonable, sensible, thinking adults. Good job he didn't know I was a boozer on the mend!

There was also a hard, determined streak to his nature. He bared his teeth in dealing with the Berndt Schuster situation at the time when the German was the biggest star by a million miles in Barcelona. Nevertheless, Terry banished him from his team in a stand that demanded a lot of courage. He had substituted Schuster in the European Cup Final and poor old Berndt got the needle with him for it. Instead of hanging around for the rest of the team at the end of the game he disappeared. As far as Terry was concerned the decision was made. He went for Gary and myself and publicly made it clear that Schuster no longer figured in his planning. But the trouble wouldn't go away. And the longer Schuster stuck to his contract the worse it got.

When things didn't work out with me the whole affair was used as a weapon against Terry. I suspect he paid for his stand on a point of principle, but at least it showed what he was made of. There was another insight into what really makes him tick when he showed interest in signing me again after he had joined Spurs. After my failure with him the first time, most managers would have been running in the opposite direction at the mere mention of my name, but not Venners. He would have taken the challenge on board again and relished it. I decided, though, that it was too risky. For us to team up at White Hart Lane would have piled too much pressure on the pair of us. So I killed the idea stone dead before it could ever really develop.

Terry's man management, knowledge of football, and invaluable experience abroad surely make him an outstanding candidate as a future manager of England. I suppose that possibility will be dictated by his success record at Spurs. But he is very much a players' manager and I can see him ending up among the silverware again. He's definitely made of the right stuff to fight for his country on the football fields of the world. The actual decision of whether he makes it rests, of course, with the men at Lancaster Gate.

Alex Ferguson, the boss who brought me back to United, has already sampled the demands of international football with Scotland. Now I believe he has one blinkered objective – to bring the First Division championship to Old Trafford. And I for one am backing him to do it. I don't think I have ever seen a single individual so fired-up and committed to one target. He wants the title so badly it hurts.

Fergie, in fact, was one of the key factors in my decision to return to United. I always wanted to come back to Britain, that's true, but the big question was where and when. He answered both points. I was still at Bayern Munich, rebuilding my confidence and career, when he flew across to convince me that my next destination had to be Old Trafford. All I can say is that he could sell ice cubes to Eskimos! His sales pitch was brilliant – and he meant every word. It was that deep conviction to the United cause that swayed me. Maybe he hasn't been at the club all that long, but he's a very definite convert. In Fergie's eyes there is nowhere else to be in the whole football world, that's how much it matters to him.

He is a very down-to-earth type of manager, although we sometimes see him flying at 5000 feet! That's when his single-minded intensity for putting United at the top of the pile comes to the surface. And then everybody in throwing distance had better duck. When Fergie has a verbal blast it can be measured on the Richter scale – and I must admit I have witnessed a few. They are something else. If you don't perform out on the park you are a likely candidate for the blow-torch treatment, either at half-time or when the final whistle goes.

I don't bellyache about it, but I suppose you have to be careful which individual is in the firing line. Some people go into their shell when they get an earfull of the boss. Me – I think it can be of benefit in shaking players up. My attitude is to get out there and, even if I believe the rollicking is a bit of an injustice, show him what I'm made of. Two goals are always better than two fingers in my book.

So far, though, I haven't been around when the dressing room has been temporarily employed as a missile testing site for the furniture industry and furniture has literally flown. But some of the other lads have been closer to the action. They have given eye-witness accounts of Fergie in such a fury that the tea cups have suddenly been launched into orbit.

I don't doubt their accounts. He is such a winner that he won't allow losing to enter his mind. He absolutely hates the word and will do almost anything to avoid it. In training Fergie has even been known to cheat to get the right result. You could say the boy's a natural twister! Actually it's more a case of bending the rules so he ends up on the victory rostrum. And he does it with such an honest look on his face. On our recent trip to the Far East there was a classic case. He set up a game of head tennis at the end of one training session. The gaffer was obviously feeling energetic, even though the rest of us were completely clapped out – and he probably knew as much, too.

It was supposed to be a one set game. His team lost. Halfway through it Jim Leighton, our goalkeeper, and one of the gaffer's team-mates, accidentally clashed in going for the same ball. Fergie was ready to send for the firing squad and the air was blue. But worse was to come. The manager lost. Guess what – we had to play *another* game. In fact he was prepared to stay on that pitch for another week until he had won. We staged a walkout until he threatened us with fines. And he was in an absolute rage when we played on – blindfolded and on one leg. But he got his way and won. So we were then, and only then, allowed to clamber back on the team bus and get to our beds at the hotel. He's some man!

It's that fiercely competitive streak that I believe will take United to the title while he is in charge. I certainly hope so, because that's the whole reason why I am back where I belong. I accept that Fergie has got a very difficult job. It's three decades since United lifted that famous trophy and it doesn't get any easier as the years trickle by. In fact that only creates additional pressure and makes it even tougher. But I genuinely feel he can answer the ultimate championship question for United. I wouldn't have returned otherwise. And when he breaks the duck once, I am also certain that a few more championships will be heading our way. The breakthrough is the critical test for us after all those seasons of failure.

Under him you have to be strong both physically and mentally. It's important to him that if the game gets tough, the toughs in his teams get going. But Fergie is also very conscious of United's heritage and that he must have players who can really play as well. His reputation as a hard-line disciplinarian is well recorded. All I can say is it's all true. He just won't stand for anybody getting out of order. You must toe the line – or else it's whack and the whole world suddenly falls on your head. Sure enough he rants and raves at times. Most of it, I suspect, is to get rid of his own pent-up frustration and anger. But if he does say something on the spur of the moment that later he regrets he is the first to mention it. I don't think he harbours grudges.

When we faded from the scene last season it hurt him badly and he let us know it. Within four days we were finished as a League force – losing down at Norwich and then we went out in the Cup to QPR. Flattened completely – for the next four months it was a disaster. In that situation Fergie had every right to be furious. He won't stand for that happening again and we all know it. He wants to be a part of history and he demands the championship more than anybody at United. And I mean everybody.

Mike England, the manager involved in my international career longer than anybody else, didn't prove himself a winner with Wales. But there is one lasting record probably worth just as much to him. He is, without any doubt, the one boss in my experience who has never had an enemy in his own dressing room. I have never known anybody more liked by most of his players, most of the time, than Mike the gentle giant. I have never heard a bad word said against him. Not in anger anyway. There might have been a bit of banter and mickey-taking after his team talks. Within the Welsh camp, believe me, they were legendary. Not so much a breakdown on the opposition as a laugh-in.

Mike was a great bloke, but his strength was clearly not standing in front of a packed dressing-room and laying it on the line. He would get names wrong, make a complete hash of the rival team, and the real hoot was his rundown for his own men. Word for word, it would be the same instructions for all the players in every single game we played. 'Neville,' he would say, 'just go out there and do what you normally do.' It might not seem funny in cold, black print but when you have heard the same spiel umpteen times it is hilarious. We would all just crack up.

No, Mike was never the finest football manager in tactical terms. He would be the first to admit it. Sure, he knew the game – after all, he had been a very good player for Wales himself. But his great strength was team loyalty. He had all the players in his pocket. They would go to hell and back for him, we all supported him to the hilt. Every last one of us was fully aware of the battles he fought on behalf of the team and of the fact that he risked his own security into the bargain. Nothing infuriated him more than our image as Ragbag Rovers. He used to go to war with the administrators about it. The whole international operation left us completely embarrassed. For a start the kits they gave us were outrageous. Tattered and torn, about five years old, some of the shirts shrunk so much they were up around the armpits, reds, greens, all different colours. It was a joke. I remember in Scotland before a World Cup game we crossed paths with their international youth team. There couldn't have been a bigger contrast. They were immaculate. Brand-new Umbro gear, sparkling white numbers, looking a million dollars. Out trooped us – supposedly the dragons of Wales – kitted out like a pub team from the worst part of town. That kind of thing made Mike's blood boil. There was another classic confrontation over another vital qualifier against the Scots. Mike wanted it played at Wrexham. So did all the players. We knew there we had a better chance of beating the hell out of them. But the top brass thought differently. It had to be staged in South Wales. Why – because they might get a few more thousand in the ground down there and a few more quid in the bank. It was just silly short-term thinking. Long term a place in the World Cup finals would have earned us millions.

That was the kind of thing Mike was up against all the time, and then he fell victim to the north v south syndrome that has overshadowed Welsh football for too long. It was the same old story. The people from the south would turn up for important policy meetings with their minds already made up. Instead of voting on reason – they voted on region. I suppose some critics would point to the record that we never qualified for the big one under Mike's management. That, I'm afraid, has to be put down to the players. We always fell down against the small fry when we were expected to do well.

However, it's my belief, and that of the majority of the other players, that Mike wasn't sacrificed because of results. He went as a classic victim of soccer politics. They were just waiting for him. Down the years he had ruffled a few feathers, upset the power bloc waiting in the background, and when the right moment came they were ready with the hatchet. The excuse was failure to make the finals of the European championships – but that's what it was, an excuse. His team to a man felt it was rough justice. We knew people in the Welsh FA were just waiting for the opportunity to get rid of him. There was talk of a rebellion in the dressing room, but mention of a players' strike was just the heat-of-the-moment stuff.

We all felt gutted for Mike, but there is no way any of us would have turned our backs on Wales. The strength of feeling was it was the totally wrong decision and that conclusion hasn't altered. His place has been taken now by Terry Yorath. That, in my view, is a very good appointment. It would have been wrong to have brought in Brian Clough. But I still maintain the sacking of Mike England wasn't necessary or deserved.

CHAPTER SIX

The 'Hard' Men

Just once in my life I've been running scared on a football field. And, despite the hardnut reputation draped on my shoulders by certain people, I don't mind admitting the fact. The frighteners were put on me by a couple of Italians who gave me the impression they had taken up our beautiful game for pin-money after quitting as Mafia hitmen.

It happened in Brescia, Northern Italy, on June 2nd 1988. The time and the date are simply burned in my brain – that's how terrifying an experience it was for me. And let me remind you that this particular contest was supposed to have been arranged as a prestige friendly. The Italians were simply warming up for the European Championship finals in West Germany a week later. We – that's the Wales team – were heading nowhere except on our summer holidays. Then war broke out and I was looking for a bunker! They came gunning for me from the start and they didn't need the aid of a customised violin case or a dark alley to do their shady business. Bergomi and Ferri, the hatchetmen on my tail, knew exactly what they were doing. It was absolutely crazy.

First of all I was nailed by one of this lovely pair as I went to collect a ball on an angled run. It had been hooked down the line and my concentration was total. According to the Welsh lads it was a good job it was. They reckon if I had seen the ambush coming I might have had a heart attack. It was that vicious and brutal – the worst they had ever seen, and some of them had seen plenty around the world on their football travels. All I know is that both my socks were completely shredded down the back from knee-joint to ankle. I needed a new pair before I could carry on. I might have had both my legs snapped in half with a tackle of that kind. How the hell that didn't happen I still haven't a clue. He must have got the sock-shredding act down to a fine art.

I still shudder to think that my career could have gone for a burton in a split second and I would never have known what hit me until it was too late. I just felt sick. But the heavy-mob treatment didn't end there. Next news, I was chasing a long pass down the middle of the park with goal chances very much in mind when the world suddenly went dark. Again, surprise, surprise, it was my two newly-acquired minders! As I went in for the kill the gap had got smaller and smaller. Finally there was just no way through – I was heading for something as solid as the Berlin Wall. Two elbows came jutting out like a couple of boomerangs and dear old Sparky was almost sparkout.

My eye came up as if I had been hit by Mike Tyson. I was lucky. If they had caught my nose first it would have finished up parked near my left ear. But as I staggered off the park I had a right shiner to show for my pains. In that one split-second I discovered the chilling truth about Italian defenders – they definitely like to hunt in pairs. Worse was to follow. Jumping for a high ball and just ready to lay it off later in the game I was suddenly stunned by one hell of a whack on the back of my head. In a matter of seconds I thought I had grown two heads; the mushrooming lump was that big. But then I got an insight into the peculiar mentality of these Italian thugs, because that is precisely what they are. Shortly after the game I was giving an interview to West German TV. They were looking for an opinion because Italy were due to face them in the championships.

Would you believe it, up strolled Bergomi, large as life and with a beam like he was meeting his long-lost brother, and asked me to swop shirts. For a moment I thought he might have been searching for his studs. I might have been able to help him on that score. I was covered in scars, bruises and bumps, resembling a guy who had just had an argument with a fully-loaded truck, and he was only concerned about having my shirt as a keepsake.

Maybe it was for his very own chamber of football horrors!

At the time I was convinced the vendetta was aimed strictly at scaring the living daylights out of me. You see the buzz was going round the grapevine that Juventus wanted me to link up with Ian Rush. I rapidly got the impression that the two assassins were not altogether convinced about the idea. Maybe they thought a kick where it hurts most might be the best reminder that I should stay out of their Italian backyard. The message didn't take long to sink in. If that was the general behaviour of hardnut defenders I was well out of it – for all the suitcases of lire on offer.

I consider that I don't lack personal courage on the pitch, but their gutter-level antics were just scandalous. I don't mind the hefty, crunching challenge if the ball is there to be won. But when it's sixty yards away up the park and the leg-breaker comes in I'm none too pleased. Added to that there were the usual stunts of shirt-tugging, elbow smashes, and Latin spitting campaign which really gets to the British professional. I've never come across anything so vicious and it's the one and only time in my career when I couldn't get off a pitch quick enough. Just for the record we beat them by a solitary goal – and it was Rushy, tormented by his own bitter experience in Turin, who smacked it in to savour the sweetest taste of revenge.

I've relished a few moments like that myself since maturing in a hard and bruising business where once, I am the first to concede, I was just a soft touch. Too soft at one stage, in fact, to have a hope of making it and of deserving a United wage packet. I needed some armour plating and I needed it fast. When the other street-wise kids got stuck in and I accidentally caught them with a loose boot I used to turn round and apologise! I'll bet they couldn't believe their ears. But I didn't know any better.

With that kind of attitude I was going absolutely nowhere. I had to find the cut-throat meanness to survive in soccer. And it was a footballer that few people at United will now probably remember who helped me make it. For that reason I'll always be eternally grateful to Gary Worrell. He was a tricky, awkward, ball-hugging winger who always made it hard for me when we were both still wet behind the ears, attempting to break through as teenagers.

61

One day, in a bloody-minded mood for once, I decided to do something about it.

Put short and not-so-sweet I decided to become a bit nasty and aggressive. I was so determined to get possession from him I made his training session a bit of a nightmare. I really got stuck in to him. It worked, too. I loved the physical contact and, just for a change, ending up with the ball. Wherever Gary is now, he probably has long forgotten what was, for him, a minor incident. But it was the major turning point in my life. From that morning kick-about I was a changed man. I got stuck into everything that moved, legitimately of course, and suddenly I started making progress through the United ranks.

Now the rough-house aggression is a natural and fundamental part of my game. It's a significant part of what makes me tick on a football pitch. Years ago, I remember, somebody mentioned another aggressive player, Mike Summerbee, who earned his corn across the road at Manchester City. Apparently, so I'm told, Mike's basic philosophy was to kick the defender first because he was always going to kick you at some stage. I'm not quite like that, but I do believe I have a right to some sort of protection from the intimidators and kick-first merchants. In other words, I can look after myself when it gets nasty. I'm lucky because I have got the physical capability to do it. At one stage I was the original nine-stone weakling and only about five feet six into the bargain. These days I feel I can handle myself with the toughest customer.

The bottom line is that I don't like great, hulking back-four players walking the earth with the conviction they can get away with murder out on the park. In fact I just don't accept it at all. I regard it as an insult when they try and whack me all over the place. I have never looked on myself as part of the gun-slinger syndrome ... the hardest man in town. That's not a part of my nature. But I do instinctively take exception to the intimidation.

Early in my United career, about the fifth or sixth senior game it would be, I got my first taste of it. All I was guilty of was trying to make myself useful and put myself about in a battle with Spurs. Little Stevie Perryman and his mate Paul Miller didn't appreciate my style at all. Soon they were into the verbals. Threatening to break me in half, and that sort of thing. And I had always believed Steve was such a polite little chap! They were probably thinking they would put this young whipper-snapper in order before he got too big for his boots. I just ignored them. In turn they got more angry with me by the minute. That was the first lesson I learned at the top. Keep your mouth shut because the people doing all the talking are really the losers.

But that doesn't mean I can't be provoked into action I might regret later. I just won't tolerate markers taking liberties with me, or my team-mates for that matter. And I am firmly convinced that defenders get the best part of the bargain as far as match officials are concerned. It seems to me that they are allowed two or three whacks at an opposing forward before the ref steps in and maybe dishes out a well-deserved booking. Let a front man take a swing with a stray boot and there's no second chance. No reprieve. It's a case of 'what's your name, son?' and you are in the black book in no time.

With me I suspect there is an added handicap. Rival players realise I have powerful legs and am probably physically stronger than a lot of forwards. So they consider they have a licence to lean on me even more heavily than the rest. Because of this they tend to whack me harder and when I don't crumple, go down and start squealing they tend to get away with it. Yet the fact that I am capable of taking the punishment better than others doesn't make it any less of a foul. It hurts me just as much. But I grit my teeth and try not to show it. You can't allow the so and so's to think for a split-second that they might be winning.

Okay, a few have got to me and provoked a reaction, I accept that. A classic case was a monster of a man called Guido Buchwald. He's built like a brick outhouse and I bumped into him for the first time when I played for Bayern Munich. Guido is a West German international and obviously very proud of the fact. Any time he wants I can certainly give him a written testimonial to his physical strength. Maybe even a medical certificate to go with it – mine! I had to tangle with Buchwald when he was playing the part of Rambo in the heart of Stuttgart's strongman defence.

The week before I had just made my debut with Bayern. Not

bad either. For once all the headlines were on my side. The German nation seemed to be nice and friendly and also on my side. Guido was the exception. He must have hated me – or so it seemed once the ball was dropped in the middle. Definitely, for the sake of Aryan pride, he was out to prove he could conquer the world or, at the very least, put me in my place. To be honest I didn't really get a kick unless it was from good old Guido's size-12 planted where it hurts most. He came straight through me like a bulldozer four, five, six times. I thought I was very hard done by, but the referee did absolutely nothing. I don't know why I even expected protection. I was a foreign player and abroad that means you get absolutely zilch.

For Buchwald, paid to stop me at all costs, it was a good day's business. I collected the bruises and then another kick in the teeth. He went public and declared that if I was supposed to be a world-class player he didn't care much for the rankings. Or something along those lines. Next time, I swore to myself, I would be ready for him. The inevitable showdown just happened to be my final, farewell game for Bayern. The last game of the German League season. Clearly the script hadn't changed for him.

Once again he hit me as hard as he could. Four or five times straight through. Next time I was ready and waited. As he flattened me I jack-knifed around and just booted him. He rolled over and there was a bit of scramble between us. I agree it deserved a booking. You can't start blatantly kicking opponents out on the park. But Buchwald had deliberately gone out to stir up a confrontation, as I saw it, and nothing happened to him. Me – I was sent off instantly. It still rankles with me. In my eyes it has tarnished a few special months in Munich. I still feel bitterly disappointed that I should have left them walking off the field for an early bath.

I don't often fall for the three card trick like that even though I have crossed swords with a few of the well-known hardmen in the British game. Right now I reckon there are not too many who truly fill the description that the likes of Tommy Smith, Norman Hunter, Peter Storey and Nobby Stiles made famous. The team's

Contemplating my future – or lack of it – in Spain   *Photo: Bob Thomas*

With Jill and the car I was so promptly given at Bayern Munich

Photo: Sunday Mirror

Training with the Bayern squad

Photo: Sunday Mirror

Getting in a shot for Wales in a European Championship qualifier against Czechoslovakia, Wrexham

Against Czechoslovakia again, this time in Prague   *Photo: Action Images*

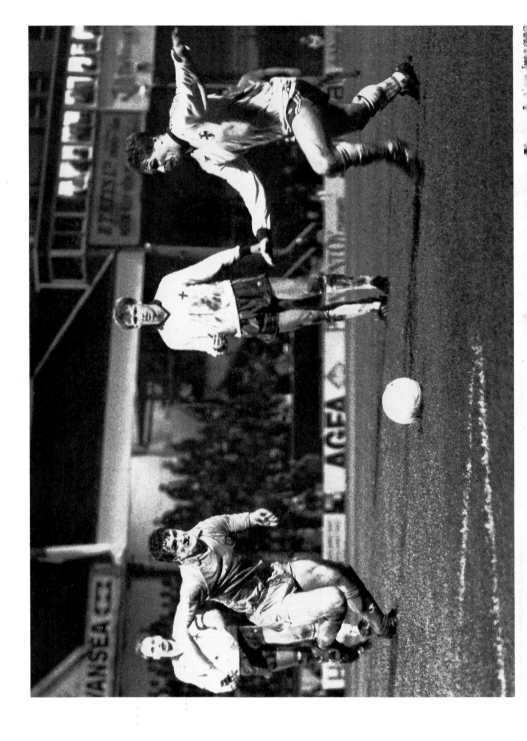

Rush and myself celebrate one of the Welsh goals, the match ended 2–2

Photo: Action Images

Mike England, manager for a large chunk of my Welsh career

Photo: Action Images

One of my "hardmen" Guido Buchwald, caught grappling with yours
truly!   *Photo: Action Images*

Paul McGrath

Bryan Robson

Mike Duxbury – four of my Man Utd "select" eleven

Photos: Action Images

Jim Leighton

There's nothing like scoring a goal ...   *Photo: Allsport*

... although being voted Players' Player of the Year 1989 isn't bad!

Photo: Bob Thomas

Photo: Daily Mirror

Photo: Daily Mirror

With Jill and new baby son Alex

Photo: Allsport

In action last season (1988/89) against Spurs

minder – the footballer always ready, waiting and willing to sort out the opposition if they wanted a rough-house.

But Jimmy Case, formerly of Liverpool and now Southampton, can definitely be billed alongside the old brigade as a player feared throughout the land. Very definitely a tough customer – the hardest case of the lot in my opinion. Aggression, strength and a natural expertise for saving his own skin are all part of Jimmy's make up. I accept that since the days Hunter was on the prowl, along with the old Anfield iron, Smithy, things have changed. The clean-up in football, with sterner enforcement of the rules, has sorted out a lot of the old problems. But I have always believed there has to be a physical, competitive edge otherwise it would never be the spectacle it is. I'm not talking about the naughty bits. You can always do without the nasty, over-the-top stuff that actually threatens the livelihood of players. But tough, uncompromising men are always welcome in my idea of football.

Jimmy is the classic example. You know if you get close to him, too close, you can get hurt. The few times I have dropped into United's midfield I have had a reminder from him that there is going to be no messing about. And I have collected a kick for my troubles. Nothing really vicious, just a reminder that he is there and you are on his patch. Nail him just once and it never leaves your mind that he will get you back. Given time, it's a promise that Casey will have his revenge. But you have to respect him as well. Not only can he look after himself, he can also play. He will destroy you with the ball as well as the boot. You don't collect all the game's top prizes, as he did at Anfield, without having exceptional, skilful qualities. Casey has hurt me a few times, and some of my mates a lot more, but you still have to have a sneaking admiration for the man.

Another classy operator with the killer touch out of the Liverpool stable was Graeme Souness. Smooth and deadly, that was his code. He could play like a dream, but step on his toes and he could turn into a living nightmare. I once saw him in action against a mate of mine, Peter Nicholas – another guy who could handle himself – when we took on Scotland in a World Cup qualifying game. I can tell you it wasn't very pretty.

As I saw it, Peter went into make a challenge on Souness. He obviously didn't like it because, while Nicko was still on the deck, Graeme just backheeled him straight in the face. A bit out of order, really.

My reading of it was that he probably recognised Nicholas as the tough guy of the Welsh team and made sure he sorted him out early. He clearly aimed to get the pecking order laid down before any of the real nonsense blew up. It was like the law of the jungle – a bit too callous for me. But I think all great players have that vital mean streak on the field. And Souness certainly had it. He was the minder of the Liverpool team for years. Let anybody step out of line in the opposition ranks and Anfield didn't have to whistle up Graeme. He was there already. Everybody knew what to expect if they tried to transform the game into a blood bath: there was only one winner. But Souness, for all his ruthless approach, was world-class in terms of technique. He had the ability to win a game on his own – and that's a very rare quality.

Another of the breed is Graham Roberts, who Souness signed from Tottenham as one the first high-priced Anglos he employed to make Glasgow Rangers a force throughout Europe. He is now handling the hit-man trade down at Stamford Bridge with Chelsea.

This particular Graham is another fierce, uncompromising character and I have had a few run-ins with him. I suppose when he meets a player like myself it's inevitable it turns into a head-to-head personal contest. He loves a scrap, that's for sure. He will kick you without batting an eyelid, but whack him back and there is not a murmur. He is not a screamer. And what I like about Graham is that he is the first ready with a handshake when all the bullets have stopped flying. I think that's very important in this game.

Norman Whiteside, until the summer of 1989 my team-mate at United, is another player who can really look after himself. Unfortunately, that image has worked against him and turned him into a 'Public Enemy No 1' personality. Nothing could be further from the truth. It draws unfair attention to him and referees now appear to be gunning for big Norman. Perhaps, and it would be a crying shame if it happened, he might have to curb his natural aggression to avoid such type-casting. And when that happens it can seriously damage your natural game.

Certainly he is a hard man, but Norman's genuine toughness is in taking punishment without a whimper, rather than dishing it out. He's got a bad name he doesn't deserve and it has stuck. But he gets more bad tackles coming his way than he ever makes himself. The reputation has been like a wanted notice around his neck, but I can vouch for Norman's skill. As a schoolboy, he was going on thirteen and looking twenty. But even more unbelievable was his ability. He used to run the show and looked in a different league from the rest of us. He can still do the same at senior level and has the medals to prove it. At Anfield they will never forget his appearance a couple of years ago when he appeared as a sub and dragged United back from certain defeat – frightening Liverpool's players half to death in the process.

I mentioned my international buddy Peter Nicholas earlier on – and how he came unbuckled against Souness. But that doesn't happen very often because he can certainly take care of himself in most situations. He has a tremendous passion for the Welsh national team. Just before a match he is in the dressing room revving up the rest of the players. You know he is going to give 200% of himself and, as soon as the whistle goes, is ready to sort a few people out.

The Welsh method is based mostly on the physical side of the game. We haven't the same amount of skill as the rest of the top teams, so we go out to smother and stifle rivals with our application, workrate and aggression. Leading us into battle is Nicholas. I'll never forget the European Championship qualifier against Denmark with Nicko. They still show it on the box and the short-run TV clip is very good knockabout entertainment! There Peter the Great is, going hell for leather to win possession, with at least five Danes sprawled in a heap at his feet. It was just like something out a skittle alley. And he is still looking at his victims as if to say, if they want any more they can have it.

Fair enough. He is ready to take it too. Just recall the Souness incident. Peter never said a word about it. But if it had happened when he was much younger it might have led to the declaration of the Third World War. He has calmed down since those headstrong early days. Maybe the same has happened to Andoni Goiccochea. Nobody should forget him. He earned the blood-red title of the Beast of Bilbao when he locked horns with Maradona in a tackle that shook the world.

Now that was an horrific challenge. True enough, the Spaniard is not the bonniest looking bloke in the world either. He has a big lantern jaw and for a minute you reckon the bolt has dropped out of his neck. But from my experience the X-rated reputation he earned in Spain is way out of line. I played against him three or four times. Always he was reasonably fair. A few whacks came my way, admittedly, but nothing too scandalous. Just a few smacks from behind, that's all. Come to think of it, maybe he didn't consider he had to put himself about against me because of the way I was playing at the time for Barcelona. Maybe I didn't warrant special treatment!

Last but not least in my roll-call of football's hardest men is an unlikely candidate, Bryan Robson – Skipper of England and my own club captain at United and a name not usually associated with this side of the game. Understandably, too. But he is the genuine article. Hard but fair. The reason I say that is because of the way Robbo tackles. It's like being hit by a runaway train, there is so much pace and power in his technique. He tackles with unbelievable speed, launching himself at the target from at least a ten yard range. Anybody else would end up flat on their face because the timing would be all wrong. Robbo doesn't ever. He just leaves the victim sprawled flat out like a burst paper bag. Now that is my idea of a hardman.

CHAPTER SEVEN

Man. Utd. All Time Greats

Draw up any of United's all-time great teams and bang in the middle of it would surely be the name Bryan Robson. He just couldn't be left out. Even now he deserves his own very special pedestal at Old Trafford, ranking equally alongside those legendary names of the recent past, Bobby Charlton, Denis Law and George Best. But once the day dawns – and I believe it will soon – that Robson banishes a billion heartaches and wins the championship that United have chased for so long, he will tower over even that incredible trio. Aye, in my opinion, he will be recognised and acknowledged as possibly the greatest of the lot. That's how highly I rate Robbo – the perfect jewel in any football crown.

Others are likely to disagree with a fair amount of fury over that kind of assessment, and I'm not looking for a verbal war, so I will stick strictly to my idea of United's best ever team. Only this one is based purely on the big names I have watched, admired and sometimes played alongside during my ten years at the club. I expect the privileged in the posh seats, as well as the fanatics on the terraces, won't all agree with my final choice but here goes ... with my own favourite side:

Jim Leighton; Mike Duxbury, Paul McGrath, Martin Buchan, Arthur Albiston; Remi Moses, Ray Wilkins, Bryan Robson; Steve Coppell, Joe Jordan, Lou Macari. Substitutes: Kevin Moran, Gordon Strachan.

And with the team-sheet pinned firmly on the wall I'll explain why each individual grabbed my vote while other obvious crowd favourites have been ignored. With apologies from me, naturally.

I can't see, for a start, how Robson can possibly be ignored as the captain – to command, bully and inspire any United side you care to declare. The man is purely and simply a giant. Down through the decades of history in the modern game, not many individuals have emerged who are capable of changing the course of a match singlehanded. Robson is one of that elite band. Take a glance in his direction and you immediately see why. When Robson is firing on all cylinders a team appears fuel injected. The difference stands out a mile if he is not quite in shape, or is carrying a knock. Like Dave Mackay in the sixties and United's own Duncan Edwards even before that, he has the high-powered leadership quality to grab football by the scruff of the neck, shake it and get the result he wants.

At both club and international level Robson's reputation is underlined as the individual always able to force the best out of his team-mates. He can do it in two ways: either by his own courage for the charge and over-the-top example; or by the kind of verbal rocket you don't want to face too often. When Robbo is angry, demanding more and not getting it, the result can feel like being on the receiving end of a blow torch. He really lets fly and the target doesn't matter – big name or small. I know because I have suffered out on the field when things have been going wrong. Mostly he will have a go at players he knows can offer more. And you can't really argue with his judgement or his actions. The truth is that what he demands of any individual, he is totally prepared to give himself. Often more besides. I don't think I have ever seen anybody braver in the whole of world football.

His personal courage out on the pitch is quite staggering. And, in a way, it has brought him some harsh and unfair criticism. For two or three years Robbo was being laid up by very serious injuries. His dislocated shoulder became a weekly headline at one stage. But he didn't deserve the sniping that went with it; the conclusion that he was something of a football crock. The crucial factor in it all is that Robson was only ever hurt because he put

70

himself at the highest risk through sheer bravery. Death-or-glory is the gospel for him. Not many players would even contemplate some of the acts of courage he considers as just part of the routine of football life.

I won't ever forget the dramatic Cup game against QPR when our manager, Alex Ferguson believed that Bryan might have broken his neck in attempting to get a result for United. I'm not surprised that that was the thought that flashed through his mind either. When it happened I was nearest to the collision zone. Robbo went up in a bone-jarring challenge with Rangers' Danny Maddox. The ball flew just wide of the post off his head, but by that time Bryan was out for the count. He was certainly unconscious even before he thundered to the deck like a rag doll. I've never witnessed anything like it. In less than five seconds Robson just went slate grey. I for one feared the worst for him. But the man is amazing, almost a walking miracle. Within a day or so he was demanding to play again. He then played on in the United cause although he was enduring dizzy spells and pain out on the pitch. And that situation went on for four or five months.

Hand on heart, I would never have done that. Neither would too many other players. But that, I suppose, is what makes him a footballer of a different breed.

The factor that strikes you first is the combative streak. Nobody wants to win more than he does. It burns him up. He has had chances to leave United, even go for the big bucks abroad, but he has stayed because he is so desperate for the First Division championship. The lasting impression, however, is that for all his fame and fortune he has remained the same. It's no secret that Robson is a very wealthy man, but there are definitely no airs and graces about him. Some players who have achieved about a tenth as much in the game strut about as though they own the world. He's just ordinary – until you meet him on a football field. Then he is very special.

Behind him I would have another strong personality. He's the goalkeeper Jim Leighton. Quiet, tough, organised and very much the professional. The game used to have a laugh at the expense of Scottish 'keepers down the years. They were the butt of all the best jokes, lying in third place behind mothers-in-law and the Irish. But Jim has nailed the whole idea as a myth. I have got to admit my judgement of 'keepers isn't based on any great knowledge of the techniques of the job. I have one basic rule – how hard are they to beat and score a goal past. Jim is very tough. The angles are always right, the ball very rarely rolling in the net. That is what you want from the last line of defence. But from Leighton there is a lot more besides – such as experience and rock-solid ability.

More than anything he possesses the confidence and know-how to sort out the men in front of him in any given situation. He's the boss in the box – a good talker who gets his team-mates in the right positions at set-pieces to sort out the opposition. It might surprise a few people that I have made Jim my No 1 because I haven't shared a dressing room with him too long. I played, in fact, a lot longer with the likes of Chris Turner and Gary Bailey. Chris also impressed me as a 'keeper, but he lacked a few inches to dominate the close-in areas under the bar when a lot of bodies piled in for the kill. In my experience it never proved a real embarrassment to him. I suspect, though, that was the basic reason why he left United.

Bailey, too, was a fantastic shot stopper. Perhaps the best I have ever seen or faced. His reflexes were phenomenal at times and saved the team on countless occasions. But, in my book, Gary had a weakness. His defenders were never quite sure of his course of action when the pressure was on. As far as covering and the like he was red-hot; working out the crosses and coming for them was certainly *not* the strongest part of his game. He lacked the command of the area that Leighton demonstrates and wasn't as good at organising a team where it really mattered.

The best 'keeper I have ever played with – or against – is Neville Southall, my international team-mate with Wales and the man I found impossible to beat for years at Everton. I've also enjoyed a few months in the Bayern Munich side with Jean-Marie Pfaff, ranked the best 'keeper in the Mexico World Cup. Frankly, I never put him in such exalted company. He appeared to me just a showman, a player whose high-profile personality on the pitch guaranteed him a lot of media attention, and consequently overshadowed his real ability at that stage of his career. He had a few dodgy games and wasn't in the same street at Leighton. In my view Jim is the all-rounder, strong in all departments instead of being absolutely brilliant in a few and ropey in others. The type who regards a clean sheet as the only thing that matters in life.

Next in line is my right full-back and that has just got to be Mike Duxbury. If ever a footballer has sacrificed himself for a club it's Mickey and for that reason alone he deserves to be in my team. But there is a lot more about him too. A few years ago, remember, he secured a place in the England team and appeared to have a long-term future assured in international football. That was sadly unbuckled by a few unfortunate injuries, but he wouldn't bellyache about that – he never does. Mike's the single-minded type who never hogs the headlines and I don't think he has wanted to play for any other club than United. Sometimes, I suspect, he has paid the price for being a highly adaptable footballer, capable of operating in several defensive and midfield roles. It's cost him his place and even then he has not been ready to go to war. Mike, a victim of injustice as he might well have felt at times, still kept his mouth shut. There was never a song and dance from him. There's no way I could be like that, but he was just as unflappable on the park.

You blinked when he made a mistake. That's how dependable he was. Never a flair player who went dancing on a crowd-pleasing overlap, but never the type who went missing in action either. His loyalty to United has certainly cost him in the bank balance. These days players make their money by moving around. Okay, Mike has had a testimonial but he could have had a lot more a lot earlier if he had moved when the chance was there. Both Everton and Coventry wanted him. He stayed put, sacrificing so much because he was committed to the cause, and that's a sound enough motive on its own to win a place in Sparky's mob.

Just as dependable is the other full-back, the left flank man Arthur Albiston. He played for United for more than ten years and hardly missed a game until the twilight of his Old Trafford career. I learned so much from him. When I first got into the United team he was like my personal radar. Every time I made a run Arthur would find me with an inch perfect pass. It was a doddle while he was around. At times, in fact, he virtually made me take up dangerous attacking positions by shaping where he would put the ball. It wasn't telepathy, but it made the job easy for me.

Arthur was so quick at closing people down, and his balance so good, that rivals never really were able to exploit his lack of inches. I never once saw a winger give him a real chaser. Dedication was his game too. They called him Chips at United, a nickname earned in his early days for the way he devoured mountains of French fries. But when it came to the crunch Arthur was ready to make his own sacrifice. The dieting started – and worse. Even though he loved a pint or two after matches, little Chips kicked the booze into touch and went teetotal to try and prolong his future at United. I know Alex Ferguson was reluctant to let him go.

Between the two of them at the back there can only be Paul McGrath. The star with the potential for being the best central defender in the world and who, at times with United, certainly lived up to that billing. In my own mind I know for sure I have never seen anybody better. He was a Rolls Royce, oozing class so that he earned himself the nickname of Turbo. It shouldn't take too much explaining really. When he wanted to flick on the power nobody could live with him. He was lucky. He was a natural athlete with a born-in talent. But he was desperately unlucky in another way. Injuries have haunted him ever since he left Ireland at 21 to be the late-arrival superstar at United.

At one stage he was being laid up for operations on his knees every few months. And I believe that contributed so much to his well-publicised problems on and off the field. He hardly got a break from the treatment room – but missing training was probably more crucial. With time on his hands, and no immediate future in football on his mind, Paul probably enjoyed a pint or two to break the boredom. Maybe later he just couldn't break the habit. But it was that blessing of being a natural athlete that helped him stroll back from the casualty list so often. Let's be absolutely honest – Paul was never exactly the slave driver of the

74

training circuit. He believed in the law of least effort; with his ability he could afford to.

He might have had a few managers searching for the rope and the suicide note with a few of his football tricks, though. One of his favourites was that casual, almost arrogant backheel flick when ambushed by four opponents inside his own box. Paul didn't attempt it to be flash. He had so much skill it seemed the perfectly natural thing for him to do. Only the boss didn't understand. I remember Ron Atkinson called him Dolly Daydream because of his laid-back style. But he also appreciated his quality. The big feller could play defence, midfield, up front – but in my team he is at centre back.

Right alongside is a completely different personality. Martin Buchan, even though I never had the privilege of playing in the same side, was somebody who terrified me. When he was at the club I was just a grateful, errand-running apprentice. He was the captain and, make no mistake about it, everyone of us knew it. To be honest, facing Martin was like dealing with an officer in the army. My knees trembled when I saw him.

In the dressing room he was always the last to change and, knowing our true station in life, we would wait patiently just to collect his crumpled up towel. He had a few idiosyncracies as well. One I remember is that Martin always had brand-new bootlaces before every game. Definitely one from the old school. When I saw him he was getting towards the end at United but you could still see the pedigree. He was without question the master of his defensive territory. Buchan wasn't the beefed-up battler who crunched rival strikers. He had the much subtler touch of the match reader and interceptor. A very polished performer and, from what people have told me around Old Trafford, the best defender out of Scotland in at least 20 years.

I've already declared that the midfield cornerstone – and skipper – can't be anyone other than Robson. He represents the powerhouse of the side, but Bryan never shrank from applauding his playmaking partner, Ray Wilkins. Neither do I. Inside the dressing room he was known as Razor, but he was never a cut-throat operator as far as the rest of us were concerned. Just the opposite in fact. When I first moved into the first-team ranks Ray was the player who really helped me to settle down. Nothing showy, but a comforting and helpful word here and there – both on and off the pitch. He made sure he had time for the rookies and, on reflection, it was probably because he had also emerged as a very young player of 17 at Chelsea.

When you're just a kid the bright lights of the First Division can appear more like third-degree spotlights. It needs time and understanding to adapt. Ray clearly understood the problems. I never understood why, but he was labelled The Crab – a nickname which brought him much criticism, and even threatened his place in the team. Supposedly, it was all because of his passing style in midfield. As far as I could see it was just cruel and unfair. But he walked through that particular wall of fire without apparently being singed by the experience. It demonstrated his tremendous depth and strength of character. In the end he had converted the once-howling terraces and before he left for Italy United's fans hailed him as Player of the Year.

They loved him at AC Milan too. I remember facing him in a pre-season tournament out there a few summers ago. At the time Ray was reaching the end of his Italian contract, but he remained a big favourite with their fans. No wonder. In that particular competition he was by far the best player on the park. The French club Paris St. Germain didn't fail to notice his midfield impact. Within a week or so – after he had embarrassed their own men on the field in Italy – they had bought him. Since then, of course, he has become 'McWilkins of Glasgow Rangers'. Another of the highly-successful imports of Graeme Souness. Some insist that he has proved the best of the lot.

Reinforcing the other side of my midfield is a footballer you would always have by your side. When the going got tough, he got tougher than anybody. Remi Moses was certainly a character to have as an ally when you were going to war. The strong, silent type – no question. He had the next dressing-room peg to me and I really had to concentrate when having a chat with Remi. Everything was done at the level of a whisper. He had his own circle of friends and really didn't mix with footballing types. Most players were never his cup of tea – he just couldn't stand their loud, boisterous, up-front kind of behaviour. He felt they were only out seeking attention and adulation and had absolutely no time for that. But he was a fabulous player to have in your team. Alongside Robbo, Remi was one of the best tacklers I have ever clapped eyes on in my life.

He went in like a guided missile from ten yards range. Not many players had the timing or technique to line up an ambush at that sort of distance. But Remi knew exactly what he was doing. He was short on inches but was power-packed with strength. This was a player, just like Norman Hunter before him, who loved nothing better than biting a few ankles. And the kind of quiet tough guy who could and would look after himself. I've got witnesses to prove it as well, if necessary. Quite a few times, if he thought people were taking liberties at his expense, he would lay them out flat. No messing. Calm, cool and without fuss.

That was the thing with Remi. You were never quite certain in your own mind where you stood with him. Make a tasty tackle on him once too often and you were in line for a pretty sharp dig – unless you managed to duck early enough. And it wasn't just Jesper Olsen in the firing line. That headline-making incident, when Ron Atkinson was in charge, created a lot of unwelcome publicity for United. But for sure it wasn't the only time it happened. Generally bust-ups like that are soon dismissed and forgotten among the other players. Remi was always the one you wanted on your side because, if it got a bit nasty out on the pitch, he would be the first by your side offering a little bit of support!

Next in line is another on-field hardcase, Joe Jordan. Old snarler himself. With his false front teeth packed away in the top pocket Joe was like something out of a horror show for the opposition. But I loved him. He played my way and, what's more important, he couldn't play any other way. Even in training he was on the top line and ready for a riot. I have watched him rip holes in people just because they didn't deliver the right kind of ball into the box for him. He had that raw, competitive, must-win streak that made him the footballer he was. There couldn't be any half measures in his school. He would rant and rave and throw his weight about. With Joe around it was absolute carnage out on the park.

But he was very much the Jekyll and Hyde, a 24 carat, genuine article in terms of split personality. Once the boots and shorts had been slung in the corner Joe was totally different. He looked a million dollars and behaved the same way. He turned into the charmer. I liked both sides of him. Once the whistle blew he was my role model as a footballer. He wasn't really big in terms of physical size but he could turn himself into a monster and look huge. Certainly as far as the opposition were concerned.

The way he set about goalkeepers and centre-backs made me feel good. My view of defenders is well known. Generally they are bigger than forwards and love nothing better than acting the bully. When the boot is on the other foot they hate it. And arguably Joe was hated by them more than most. They reckon he perfected the art of the flying elbow. I don't know about that. What I do know is that if ever Joe got whacked himself – and many times he did quite brutally – there was never a single complaint or a moan. I suppose he was a throwback to an earlier breed of centre-forward, but he had a lot of skill as well. Joe was no mug when it came to technique. Lining up the ammunition for a warhead like Jordan, you couldn't ask for a better arms dealer than Steve Coppell. He was an absolute master of his trade. While he was still an apprentice I used to watch him from the back row of the main stand – and marvel. I wasn't alone. Dozens of other United kids did exactly the same. We used to watch and wonder over the fact that here we had an established England international, one of the world's special players, and he still worked like a dog. Coppell, as far as we were concerned, had to be bionic. He must represent the untouchable ideal of the modern winger. A supplier of crosses and danger – and a non-stop protector of defences. He was soccer's original shuttle. Nobody ever worked harder.

So many managers raise a doubting eyebrow and are critical of wingers. They suspect they offer a trick and not much else. Otherwise they don't want to know and don't get involved. But

Steve would drive himself into the ground for the sake of his team. He was a striker's dream. Eight times out of ten you get the sort of winger who drives you barmy. There you are making runs into the box, busting a gut to get on the end of a cross and score, and all he wants to do is beat the full-back, go back and beat him again – at least six times. No good for me, no good for Jordan. By the time he slings the ball in the box you have got tired of waiting and don't make the attacking run that might count for everything.

The bottom line about Steve's game was that he never fannied about like that. He got the ball across where the striker wanted it exactly and where he expected it, too. But for that kind of delivery Coppell paid a very heavy personal price. He was finished by a knee injury at just 29. With his talent he could certainly have reckoned on playing for another five years at the very least. He didn't because of his technique in crossing the ball. Steve used to whip the ball in, exerting a tremendous and damaging strain on his knee joints. It finished him early, but while he was around there wasn't a better winger to watch. Not in my book anyway.

Same size, same golden quality, same eye-catching crowd appeal – that was Lou Macari. I accept that he played a major part of his United career in midfield, but in my team he's going up front. Goalscorers like him have got to be booked a place. But he had many other assets. He was so sharp, was blessed with very quick feet, and knew the menace to defences of keeping the ball moving all the time. Look at Liverpool, they do the same. I don't think it's a coincidence they tried to sign him at the same time as United.

Lou was a tenacious battler and unbelievable in the air for a player his size. I won't ever forget that famous Cup goal he set up for Frank Stapleton by climbing above rivals twice his build. It was the strike that put us well on the road to Wembley. His impact wasn't reserved for public occasions. He could be just as devastating for the rest of us within the private confines of the club. Lou was a strict teetotaller, but he got his highs from a different direction. He was United's No. 1 mickey-taker and practical joker. There are umpteen stories still circulating of how he caused mayhem at Old Trafford with his mischief. But I was a victim only once – along with my mate Graeme Hogg, now down at Portsmouth.

The three of us had just come back from an away trip. We were still the wide-eyed kids, very much the innocents of the party. So when Lou asked us to share a taxi home we readily agreed. The only trouble was, we lived on the opposite side of town. And when we arrived at Lou's house he was out of the cab in a flash. Next problem – we were miles off our route and we hadn't a brass farthing in our pockets. What a humiliation! Two United players skint and unable to pay for the ride home. We ended up having to knock up our digs and beg the money while the driver waited outside – quietly smirking at our embarrassment. Next day Lou was waiting with a big grin all over his face – and thirty quid in his hand to give us for the taxi. We learned our lesson, but he was still pulling flankers on First Division defenders for years to come. And scoring goals.

The personality who couldn't fail to score with our fans was Kevin Moran, who had a heart as big as Killarney and is a man I couldn't possibly overlook for one of the important subs' jobs in any modern team. He was literally prepared to shed blood for the sake of United and very often did. He ended up with more stitches in his face than a road accident victim, yet it never made a scrap of difference to his commitment. Moran would have walked through a mountain if it meant three points. A measure of his determination and character was revealed in his actual signing at United as a comparatively late arrival. At the time, aged around 21, he was already established as one of the legends of Gaelic Football back in Dublin. An all-Ireland champion. To turn his back on that kind of sporting achievement to take on the risks of pro soccer says a lot about Kevin. But he had both the skill and the strength to make it, carrying his country all the way to the European Championship finals in the summer of 1988.

Not quite as big but just as gutsy is my other substitute, Gordon Strachan. He was a real imp of a footballer, who could cut you down to size with a shaft of dry humour just as quickly as he would wrong foot a full-back. He was bought in my very first season in the First Division and made a truly spectacular impact,

80

knocking in more than 20 goals. I couldn't believe he had so much magic at his feet. Later on, though, I think Gordon lost a little bit of pace. He wasn't able to get past the last man with such devastating effect. However, he remained an exceptional performer and just the ball-artist to round off my perfect United team.

CHAPTER EIGHT
Change of English Game

Back in the late seventies I remember Rodney Marsh telling the world that within ten years football would be dead and buried. He reckoned that by then it would be doomed as a grey game played on grey days. That all the ball-playing entertainers like himself would have been driven out. Scattered into oblivion.

Rodney's declared judgement day has arrived and, I'm glad to say, we have all survived. We are still very much alive and kicking. The epitaphs have not been planted nationwide just yet. But it might just be time to dig a few holes and erect some well-intentioned warning signs about the state of soccer in Britain. To point out that the best game on earth might need a bit of helpful medicine. And before too long as well. Otherwise Mr. Marsh's prophetic words might just come true.

I don't intend to provoke a national panic, but I must admit I was quite stunned and disappointed at the sudden way football had declined while I had my back turned playing abroad. Just two years with Barcelona and Bayern Munich had brought changes – for the worse I might add – that you wouldn't expect in two decades. It seemed to me that kick-and-rush ruled. Don't for a moment get the idea that this is yet another well-rehearsed attack on Wimbledon. Their dependence on and mastery of the long-ball technique has taken them a long way and brought an unfashionable club a lot of success. I'm not going to knock it. If you've unlocked a system and found it works to your advantage you're not going to chuck it in the dustbin simply because a few critics start bellyaching.

Climbing four divisions of the Football League and winning an FA Cup Final is too much of a bargain to swop for a few carping words. And, honestly, with that record I don't see Wimbledon changing now. What bothers me far more is the number of copy-cats who have seen the trick perfected at Plough Lane and decided to have a bit of the action. And that's where I really see the game going down the plughole. Fast. Instead of long-ball the plan too often turns into the crude big-boot. It was that development which really hit me between the eyes when I came home and definitely alarms me about the future of football in Britain.

In a strange sort of way, Liverpool might innocently have to carry the can for what has happened. Certainly in the First Division. No, I'm not suggesting for a moment that they trade in the aerial power game, just the opposite. Their one-touch, sweet-passing, off-the-ball running style has swept them to almost total supremacy in the last twenty years. And that's the trouble. At least for the rest of us. They have swaggered to a virtual monopoly of the championship, ruled Europe until they were banned, and had a Wembley date jotted in their diary most seasons. Great for Anfield – misery for everybody else.

A bit of a turn-off for rival managers who had to compete with a monster and knew they were invariably on a loser. Not only did the whole business drive them to despair, I suspect it also drove them to other methods. They tried, and mostly failed, to borrow Liverpool's super-slick system because they either didn't really twig the secret, or hadn't got the right players – or both. Then they had to search for another more drastic solution. They turned instead to the long-ball, a game that anybody can play if they have the basics of two legs and a pair of lungs like a blacksmith's bellows. They reckoned it would put them back in business. Short-term it just might work, but long-term it's got to be a disaster for the game. Once too many teams commit themselves to the same basic routine football will die on its feet. And after one season back with United that fear is growing at an alarming rate, to my mind.

In 1986, when I climbed aboard the plane for Barcelona, my

opinion was that the majority of England's elite clubs – those lucky enough to have Division One status – played the right way. With style, passing control, passion and a build-up from the back. Since I've got back you can probably count them on one hand. Liverpool, naturally. Then Norwich, Derby, Forest and ourselves. The rest, in varying forms, have taken the other road. Route-one football as it's called. Fear is an obvious factor in the new formula – and not just of Liverpool. Managers rely on results to keep the paycheck dropping into the bank account. Failure isn't tolerated for very long on our terraces, even in the most charitable of boardrooms.

Plonk yourself in the boss's chair and you rapidly discover the ultimatum: win or else. And with the flow of skilful players drying up – quality is a premium that costs millions – too many managers have little alternative. They compensate by drilling their players harder. Making them fitter, tougher, stronger. If you can't play, at least you can outlast, out-compete, out-run the other lot. But it's a vicious circle. The longer the philosophy persists, the further it creeps down the chain with grassroots football throwing up the same kind of young players. All out of the same mould. Brilliant athletes, true, but probably not as skilful as they used to be. When the game is all about running, you just don't have a second to catch your breath, let alone time to learn and polish technique and ball control. And time is essential in football – even at the highest level – if the entertainers are to survive.

Right now I think we are at the outer limits. The tempo can be frantic and a bit frightening, too. If we are not careful we are going to be creating a whole line of football robots. Players with all the physical power in the world and not enough skill. I've noticed the trend already. There is less space and time in and around the box now than two years ago and dramatically less than when I made my United debut. Things are changing that fast. Defenders seem to be getting bigger and quicker. If you are not six-feet-three these days you can forget a job at the back. Or that's the way it seems. Size and strength are what counts in the modern game. Unless we watch these dangerous trends it could become a game for the musclemen – a battle of the giants. I'm certainly the last player to argue against physical aggression, power play and all-out determination; they are very much a part of my football code. Coupled with the professional honesty of players over here – you don't get many cheats in our game – they are the qualities that have made us envied across the world. But obviously you can go one step too far with these basic beliefs – the fatal step of having too much of a good thing. That's when everything could come crashing down.

Some people argue that our exclusion from European competition has steamrollered our football into this new-wave of tactics. But I don't go along with the idea that it is the isolation alone which has changed the face of our game. The responsibility for it all rests with the managers and coaches. They dictate the methods and tactics, nobody else. Okay, let them argue that they haven't the raw material to do anything else, but Liverpool and a few others destroy the protest. In my opinion, it's only the managers who can effectively do anything about it right now. They have the power to halt the revolution before it is too late. We need their resolve to resist the worst aspects of the 'route-one' merchants.

I don't condemn the long-ball approach completely. Played the right way it can be very exciting, on the terraces and on the field. Players know where the ball is going to be delivered and, for forwards like myself, that is the whole secret of success. You can make positive runs with the inbuilt knowledge that you are going to get possession where it counts. Good players can make the system superb. As long as it is mixed, during the course of ninety-minutes, with football of a slower tempo when the time demands.

However, I still maintain that unless the big-boot brigade – a corruption of the original idea – are stopped here and now there is one inevitable conclusion. Football will develop into an endurance test, for players and spectators alike. And that's when Rodney Marsh's forecast might have the real ring of truth about it. For me, when football is played the right way, it still represents the greatest show on earth. Played the wrong way it deserves to be slammed and run out of town. We don't want Barnum and

Bailey out on the park, or Palladium tricks from the fancy dans, but the real entertainers have got to be given a chance of survival. Without them we might as well all stay at home.

STATISTICS –
MANCHESTER UNITED AND WALES
Compiled by Cliff Butler

Birthplace: Wrexham, North Wales
Birthdate: 1st November 1963
Signed apprentice (for Manchester United): 29th May 1980
Signed professional (for Manchester United): 1st November 1980
Transferred to C.F. Barcelona (Spain): July 1986
Transferred back to Manchester United: June 1988

MANCHESTER UNITED

Playing Career

Competition	Appearances	Goals
Football League	128 (4)	52
F.A. Challenge Cup	17	7
Football League Cup	8 (1)	4
European Cup Winners' Cup	2 (2)	0
UEFA Cup	8	2

· SPARKY ·

FOOTBALL LEAGUE APPEARANCES (MANCHESTER UNITED)
Season 1983–84

Opponents	Result	Venue
SOUTHAMPTON*	3 – 2	Old Trafford
LEICESTER CITY	2 – 0 (1 goal)	Old Trafford
ARSENAL*	4 – 0	Old Trafford
BIRMINGHAM CITY*	1 – 0	Old Trafford
NOTTS COUNTY*	0 – 1	Meadow Lane
COVENTRY CITY	4 – 1 (2 goals)	Old Trafford
WEST HAM UNITED	0 – 0	Old Trafford
EVERTON	1 – 1	Goodison Park
IPSWICH TOWN	1 – 2 (1 goal)	Old Trafford
TOTTENHAM HOTSPUR	1 – 1	White Hart Lane
NOTTINGHAM FOREST	0 – 2	City Ground

Season 1984–85

WATFORD	1 – 1	Old Trafford
SOUTHAMPTON	0 – 0	The Dell
IPSWICH TOWN	1 – 1 (1 goal)	Portman Road
CHELSEA	1 – 1	Old Trafford
NEWCASTLE UNITED	5 – 0 (1 goal)	Old Trafford
COVENTRY CITY	3 – 0	Highfield Road
LIVERPOOL	1 – 1	Old Trafford
WEST BROMWICH ALBION	2 – 1	The Hawthorns
ASTON VILLA	0 – 3	Villa Park
WEST HAM UNITED	5 – 1 (1 goal)	Old Trafford
TOTTENHAM HOTSPUR	1 – 0 (1 goal)	Old Trafford
EVERTON	0 – 5	Goodison Park
ARSENAL	4 – 2 (1 goal)	Old Trafford
LEICESTER CITY	3 – 2 (1 goal)	Filbert Street
LUTON TOWN	2 – 0	Old Trafford
SUNDERLAND	2 – 3 (1 goal)	Roker Park
NORWICH CITY	2 – 0 (1 goal)	Old Trafford
IPSWICH TOWN	3 – 0	Old Trafford
STOKE CITY	1 – 2	Victoria Ground

90

CHELSEA	3 – 1 (1 goal)	Stamford Bridge
SHEFFIELD WEDNESDAY	1 – 2 (1 goal)	Old Trafford
COVENTRY CITY	0 – 1	Old Trafford
WEST BROMWICH ALBION	2 – 0	Old Trafford
NEWCASTLE UNITED	1 – 1	St James's Park
ARSENAL	1 – 0	Highbury
EVERTON	1 – 1	Old Trafford
TOTTENHAM HOTSPUR	2 – 1 (1 goal)	White Hart Lane
WEST HAM UNITED	2 – 2	Boleyn Ground
ASTON VILLA	4 – 0 (3 goals)	Old Trafford
LIVERPOOL	1 – 0	Anfield
LEICESTER CITY	2 – 1	Old Trafford
STOKE CITY	5 – 0 (2 goals)	Old Trafford
SHEFFIELD WEDNESDAY	0 – 1	Hillsborough
LUTON TOWN	1 – 2	Kenilworth Road
SOUTHAMPTON	0 – 0	Old Trafford
SUNDERLAND	2 – 2	Old Trafford
NORWICH CITY	1 – 0	Carrow Road
WATFORD	1 – 5	Vicarage Road

Season 1985–86

ASTON VILLA	4 – 0 (2 goals)	Old Trafford
IPSWICH TOWN	1 – 0	Portman Road
ARSENAL	2 – 1 (1 goal)	Highbury
WEST HAM UNITED	2 – 0 (1 goal)	Old Trafford
NOTTINGHAM FOREST	3 – 1 (1 goal)	City Ground
NEWCASTLE UNITED	3 – 0 (1 goal)	Old Trafford
OXFORD UNITED	3 – 0	Old Trafford
MANCHESTER CITY	3 – 0	Maine Road
SOUTHAMPTON	1 – 0 (1 goal)	Old Trafford
LUTON TOWN	1 – 1 (1 goal)	Kenilworth Road
QUEEN'S PARK RANGERS	2 – 0 (1 goal)	Old Trafford
LIVERPOOL	1 – 1	Old Trafford
CHELSEA	2 – 1 (1 goal)	Stamford Bridge
COVENTRY CITY	2 – 0	Old Trafford
SHEFFIELD WEDNESDAY	0 – 1	Hillsborough
TOTTENHAM HOTSPUR	0 – 0	Old Trafford

91

LEICESTER CITY	0 – 3	Filbert Street
WATFORD	1 – 1	Old Trafford
IPSWICH TOWN	1 – 0	Old Trafford
ASTON VILLA	3 – 1 (1 goal)	Villa Park
ARSENAL	0 – 1	Old Trafford
EVERTON	1 – 3	Goodison Park
BIRMINGHAM CITY	1 – 0	Old Trafford
OXFORD UNITED	3 – 1 (1 goal)	Manor Ground
NOTTINGHAM FOREST	2 – 3	Old Trafford
WEST HAM UNITED	1 – 2	Boleyn Ground
LIVERPOOL	1 – 1	Anfield
WEST BROMWICH ALBION	3 – 0	Old Trafford
SOUTHAMPTON	0 – 1	The Dell
LUTON TOWN	2 – 0 (1 goal)	Old Trafford
MANCHESTER CITY	2 – 2	Old Trafford
BIRMINGHAM CITY	1 – 1	St Andrews
EVERTON	0 – 0	Old Trafford
COVENTRY CITY	3 – 1	Highfield Road
CHELSEA	1 – 2	Old Trafford
SHEFFIELD WEDNESDAY	0 – 2	Old Trafford
NEWCASTLE UNITED	4 – 2 (2 goals)	St. James's Park
TOTTENHAM HOTSPUR	0 – 0	White Hart Lane
LEICESTER CITY	4 – 0 (1 goal)	Old Trafford
WATFORD	1 – 1 (1 goal)	Vicarage Road

Season 1988–89

QUEEN'S PARK RANGERS	0 – 0	Old Trafford
LIVERPOOL	0 – 1	Anfield
MIDDLESBROUGH	1 – 0	Old Trafford
LUTON TOWN	2 – 0	Kenilworth Road
WEST HAM UNITED	2 – 0 (1 goal)	Old Trafford
TOTTENHAM HOTSPUR	2 – 2 (1 goal)	White Hart Lane
WIMBLEDON	1 – 1 (1 goal)	Plough Lane
NORWICH CITY	1 – 2 (1 goal)	Old Trafford
EVERTON	1 – 1 (1 goal)	Goodison Park
ASTON VILLA	1 – 1	Old Trafford
DERBY COUNTY	2 – 2 (1 goal)	Baseball Ground

SOUTHAMPTON	2 – 2 (1 goal)	Old Trafford
SHEFFIELD WEDNESDAY	1 – 1 (1 goal)	Old Trafford
NEWCASTLE UNITED	0 – 0	St. James's Park
CHARLTON ATHLETIC	3 – 0 (1 goal)	Old Trafford
COVENTRY CITY	0 – 1	Highfield Road
ARSENAL	1 – 2 (1 goal)	Highbury
NOTTINGHAM FOREST	2 – 0 (1 goal)	Old Trafford
LIVERPOOL	3 – 1 (1 goal)	Old Trafford
MIDDLESBROUGH	0 – 1	Ayresome Park
MILLWALL	3 – 0 (1 goal)	Old Trafford
WEST HAM UNITED	3 – 1	Boleyn Ground
TOTTENHAM HOTSPUR	1 – 0	Old Trafford
SHEFFIELD WEDNESDAY	2 – 0	Hillsborough
NORWICH CITY	1 – 2	Carrow Road
ASTON VILLA	0 – 0	Villa Park
LUTON TOWN	2 – 0	Old Trafford
NOTTINGHAM FOREST	0 – 2	City Ground
ARSENAL	1 – 1	Old Trafford
MILLWALL	0 – 0	The Den
DERBY COUNTY	0 – 2	Old Trafford
CHARLTON ATHLETIC	0 – 1	Selhurst Park
COVENTRY CITY	0 – 1	Old Trafford
WIMBLEDON	1 – 0	Old Trafford
SOUTHAMPTON	1 – 2	The Dell
QUEEN'S PARK RANGERS	2 – 3	Rangers Stadium
EVERTON	1 – 2 (1 goal)	Old Trafford
NEWCASTLE UNITED	2 – 0	Old Trafford

* – Substitute appearance

F.A. CHALLENGE CUP Appearances
Season 1984–85

Opponents (Round)	Result	Venue
AFC Bournemouth (3)	3 – 0	Old Trafford
Coventry City (4)	2 – 1 (1 goal)	Old Trafford
Blackburn Rovers (5)	2 – 0	Ewood Park

West Ham United (6)	4 – 2 (1 goal)	Old Trafford
Liverpool (S.F.)	2 – 2 (1 goal)	Goodison Park
Liverpool (S.F. replay)	2 – 1 (1 goal)	Maine Road
Everton (Final)	1 – 0	Wembley

Season 1985–86

Rochdale (3)	2 – 0 (1 goal)	Old Trafford
West Ham United (5)	1 – 1	Boleyn Ground
West Ham United (5 replay)	0 – 2	Old Trafford

Season 1988–89

Queen's Park Rangers (3)	0 – 0	Old Trafford
Queen's Park Rangers (3 replay)	2 – 2	Rangers Stadium
Queen's Park Rangers (3 – 2nd replay)	3 – 0	Old Trafford
Oxford United (4)	4 – 0 (1 goal)	Old Trafford
AFC Bournemouth (5)	1 – 1 (1 goal)	Dean Court
AFC Bournemouth (5 replay)	1 – 0	Old Trafford
Nottingham Forest (6)	0 – 1	Old Trafford

FOOTBALL LEAGUE CUP
(Milk Cup, Littlewoods Cup) Appearances

Season 1983–34

Opponents (Round)	Result	Venue
Port Vale (2 – 2nd Leg)*	2 – 0	Old Trafford
Oxford United (4)	1 – 1 (1 goal)	Manor Ground

Season 1984–85

Burnley (2 – 1st Leg)	4 – 0 (3 goals)	Old Trafford
Everton (3)	1 – 2	Old Trafford

Season 1985–86

Crystal Palace (2 – 2nd Leg)	1 – 0	Old Trafford
West Ham United (3)	1 – 0	Old Trafford

Season 1988–89
Rotherham United
   (2 – 1st Leg)   1 – 0   Millmoor
Rotherham United
   (2 – 2nd Leg)   5 – 0   Old Trafford
Wimbledon (3)   1 – 2   Plough Lane

* – Substitute appearance

EUROPEAN COMPETITION
Appearances Season 1983–84

European Cup Winners' Cup

Opponents (Round)	Result	Venue
Spartak Varna (2 – 2nd Leg)* (Bulgaria)	2 – 0	Old Trafford
Barcelona (3 – 1st Leg) (Spain)	0 – 2	Barcelona
Barcelona (3 – 2nd Leg)* (Spain)	3 – 0	Old Trafford
Juventus (S.F. 2nd Leg) (Italy)	1 – 2	Turin

Season 1984–85 (UEFA Cup)

Raba Vasas Gyor (1 – 1st Leg) (Hungary)	3 – 0 (1 goal)	Old Trafford
Raba Vasas Gyor (1 – 2nd Leg) (Hungary)	2 – 2	Gyor
PSV Eindhoven (2 – 1st Leg) (Netherlands)	0 – 0	Eindhoven
PSV Eindhoven (2 – 2nd Leg) (Netherlands)	1 – 0	Old Trafford
Dundee United (3 – 1st Leg) (Scotland)	2 – 2	Old Trafford
Dundee United (3 – 2nd Leg) (Scotland)	3 – 2 (1 goal)	Tannadice Park

* – Substitute appearance

· SPARKY ·

Videoton (4 – 1st Leg) (Hungary)	1 – 0	Old Trafford
Videoton (4 – 2nd Leg) (Hungary)	0 – 1	Szekesfehervar

INTERNATIONAL APPEARANCES FOR WALES

Season	Opponents	Result	Venue
1983–84	ENGLAND (BIC)	1 – 0 (1 goal)	Wrexham
	NORTHERN IRELAND (BIC)	1 – 1 (1 goal)	Swansea
1984–85	ICELAND (WC)	0 – 1	Reykjavik
	SPAIN (WC)	0 – 3	Seville
	ICELAND (WC)	2 – 1 (1 goal)	Cardiff
	NORWAY	1 – 1	Wrexham
	SCOTLAND (WC)	1 – 0	Glasgow
	SPAIN (WC)	3 – 0 (1 goal)	Wrexham
	NORWAY	2 – 4 (1 goal)	Bergen
1985–86	SCOTLAND (WC)	1 – 1 (1 goal)	Cardiff
	HUNGARY	0 – 3	Cardiff
	URUGUAY	0 – 0	Cardiff
1986–87	SOVIET UNION	0 – 0	Swansea
	CZECHOSLOVAKIA (EC)	1 – 1	Wrexham
1987–88	DENMARK (EC)	1 – 0 (1 goal)	Cardiff
	DENMARK (EC)	0 – 1	Copenhagen
	CZECHOSLOVAKIA	0 – 2	Prague
	SWEDEN	1 – 4	Stockholm
	MALTA	3 – 2 (1 goal)	Ta' Qali
	ITALY	1 – 0	Brescia
1988–89	HOLLAND (WC)	0 – 1	Amsterdam
	FINLAND (WC)	2 – 2	Swansea
	ISRAEL	3 – 3	Tel Aviv
	SWEDEN	0 – 2	Wrexham
	WEST GERMANY	0 – 0	Cardiff

BIC – British International Championship
WC – World Cup
EC – European Championship